BLYTH MEMORIES
PART FOUR

For decades Blyth Market was the biggest and best in East Northumberland but the number of stallholders has dwindled over the years. It was badly hit when it had to move temporarily to the Keel Row Mall car park when work started on refurbishing the market place and never really recovered. The brightly covered stalls provided by Blyth Council for the new market proved "not fit for purpose" as the condensation affected the goods on display. This picture taken in 1959 shows what the market was like in its hayday. The building on the left is the old Central Cinema, the Zion Church is immediately behind it and the spire of the United Reformed Church is top left. St Mary's Church can be seen in the background on the right.

Jim Harland

The development of local government in Blyth began in the 18th Century with the formation of the South Blyth Local Board which became the South Blyth Urban District Council in 1894. Twelve years later it amalgamated with Cowpen U.D.C. to form Blyth Urban District Council. This lasted until September, 1922, when it was granted the charter of a Borough. Souvenirs of the granting of the charter were printed and distributed throughout the town. The borough was in existence until 1974 when it amalgamated with Seaton Valley Urban Council to become Blyth Valley Borough Council. This authority lasted until 2009 when the two tier government system was abolished and Northumberland County Council took over the administration. A Blyth Town Council was formed but this has comparatively little power and little money.

Copyright Jim Harland 2013

First published in 2013 by

Summerhill Books
PO Box 1210, Newcastle-upon-Tyne NE99 4AH

www.summerhillbooks.co.uk

email: summerhillbooks@yahoo.co.uk

ISBN: 978-1-906721-70-1

No part of this publication may be reproduced, stored in a mechanical retrieval system, or transmitted, in any form or by any means, electronic, mechanical, photocopying, recording or otherwise, without prior permission of the author.

Contents

Introduction	4
Blyth at War – Part One	5
The Big Storm	9
The Blyth Hero	12
The End of Blyth Grammar School	14
The Blyth Squatters Battle	17
The Phoenix – The Last Theatre in Town	21
Memories of the Shipyard	24
The Newspapers of Blyth	28
The Tragedy of Blyth's Pianist Prodigy	30
The Two Strong Men of Blyth	33
Blyth's Singing Teenager	36
The Blyth Oriana Choir	39
The Youth Club Author	42
Wellesley Nautical School	46
The Music Makers of Blyth	51
Blyth's Golden Age of Youth Clubs	54
The Ferry Across the Water	59
Blyth's Olympic Boxing Coach	62
Blyth at War – Part Two	64
The Rise and Fall of the Singing Miners	66
The Seven Stars Story	68
The Big Steeple Church	69
The Scottish Fisher Girls	72

Personalities of the Town of Blyth

Bill the All-Rounder	74
Tommy Bell – Mr. Music	75
Leonora Rogers – Dancing Mistress	76
Pauline Ryder – The Landlady	76
Hoot Gibson – Cowboy Copper	78
Dorothy Hartshorne – Blyth's Bicycling Nurse	79
Black Geordie – Scary Man	80

Introduction

I am absolutely amazed at being able to produce this fourth edition of Blyth Memories. After the second edition in 2011, I doubted there was sufficient material for a third book. I was proved wrong. Thanks to the enthusiasm and keenness of many people I was able to bring out the third edition last year and now I find, again through suggestions from Blyth-born folk, that there is sufficient history in Blyth to publish a fourth. It is extremely gratifying to be stopped in the street by strangers and old friends to discuss the latest edition and to hear what they would like in future editions.

At least four of the chapters you are about to read have come from these discussions Mind you, with the aid of Gerry Evans, Gordon Smith and George Robson, I have had to turn detective and cover many miles to track down informants that can give me the facts. It is sad though to have to write of the demise about what were vital cogs in the well being of Blyth, the shipyard and the grammar school being but two.

On the other hand it was a delight to put on paper the reminiscences of folks who lived during the 1939-45 period in the town.

I also uncovered an Olympic boxing coach living in retirement in Cowpen Estate and a Blyth sailor buried in a Tripoli grave twelve months after getting a medal only surpassed by the Victoria Cross.

In 2013 there has been criticism of Blyth from both in and out. A council leader being disparaging about the town he lives in and two television programmes about the independent lifeboat which certainly did not show us in a good light. It is pleasing, however, to write for posterity the amazing, excellent things that have happened in Wor Toon.

Jim Harland
Blyth 2013

Acknowledgements

Gerry Evans, Dorothy Hartshorne, Fred Moffatt, Gordon Smith, Johnny Stenhouse, Gordon Young, Phil Rawstone, News Post Leader and Rosemary Harland.

Front Cover

Top picture: Blyth Bus Station in 1959. On the left of the picture fronted by a hedge is the public toilet which was permanently manned although no charge was levied. Behind is the T. & B. Garage eventually demolished along with the Theatre Royal to make way for the Mall car park. The tall structure is part of the gas works and top right is the short-lived Roxy Cinema, now a bingo hall. The bus is the service 7 direct to North Shields Ferry. Nowadays it's a two bus trip changing at Whitley Bay.

Bottom picture: Schools football between the wars was extremely popular and attracted large crowds. Blyth was no exception and thanks to the enthusiasm and support of a large number of senior figures junior soccer thrived in the town. It was highly organised as is proved by this photograph of the 1935-36 team and officials. The goalkeeper was Harry Mills who was to go on to be a long serving player for Huddersfield Town and the youngster wearing his Northumberland cap was Stan Riddell. Another allround sportsman – golf, cricket, snooker and soccer – was Bill Emery seen here with his hands on his hips. Back row: J. Pearson (secretary Blyth Schools F.A.), J. Hooper, B. Coulson, Harry Mills, W. "Danny" Dawson (chairman Blyth Schools F.A.), Bill Emery. Middle row: Ald. T.C. Blackburn (President), W. Milburn, T. Downie, R.S. Wilson, R.R. Walton, F. Mitchell and R.W. Robertson. Front row: G. Hudson, J.F. Herrwick, F.A. Chapple, Coun. J.W. Heatley (Mayor of Blyth), Stan Riddell, Ald. J.J. Reilly, N. Brannigan, J. Thompson and D. Lake.

Blyth at War – Part One

Campers fleeing to the sand dunes at Blyth at the sound of the first air raid siren, the reindeer rescued from Norway by a submarine and six skeletons found after the war thought to be submariners who had gone out for a walk but posted as absent without leave, all stories fascinating told by a Blyth woman who lived the five years of the Second World War in the middle of a militarised zone.

The woman is Margaret Gilhespy, who, with her brother Alan, were the offspring of Ned and Elsie Gilhespy who ran a market garden next to their home, Link House Gardens opposite Blyth Links, and adjoining Link House and Link House Farm. Margaret, now 87 and living in retirement in the Northumberland village of Humshaugh, trained as a nurse in Newcastle before working in Edinburgh for 23 years as a nurse and health administrator. She then lived and worked in America and in various cities in England before coming back to the North East. In all she spent 43 years in her career but never returned to her home town other than a brief visit in the 1990's. She wrote her memories in 2002 at the request of Mark Wood, Lord Ridley's agent, who was compiling information and seeking historical pictures of the Blyth area. She passed it on to the agent who, in turn, eventually gave it to Blyth Borough Council. It was retrieved when the council was abolished. This is an abridged version of her writings.

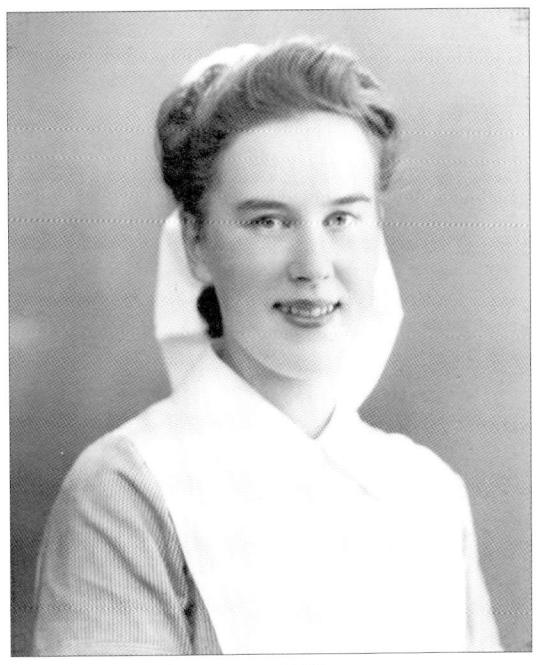

* * * * * * * * *

Margaret Gilhespy.

I don't imagine many families spent the six years between 1939 and 1945 living between the Wellesley Nautical School and Gloucester Lodge Farm surrounded on three sides by HM forces. Visiting that area today it is almost impossible to visualise it as it was in my childhood. There are big roads, roundabouts, hundreds of uninteresting small houses and, of course, horrendous traffic.

Then it was a very rural area. There were neatly trimmed hawthorn hedges and wild flowers in small fields, the burn running in front of the house where my brother Alan and I fished for minnows.

My father developed a camp site and families, mostly from Tyneside and Wearside and without cars, came every weekend by bus, motor cycle and even bicycle. Hundreds of tents were pitched and my mother opened a small hut as a shop. Although having no experience as a shopkeeper she did quite well stocking paraffin oil, tea, sugar, tinned beans and packets of biscuits.

Of course her own fresh laid eggs were popular as was bread provided by a local baker. Most of the campers cooked on a single ring oil stove so their needs were simple. There was an old radio in the hut and I was there, surrounded by campers, at eleven o clock on Sunday, September 3rd., 1939, when the Prime Minister, Neville Chamberlain, made the famous broadcast that "This country is now at war with Germany."

Almost immediately we heard the air raid sirens wailing for the very first time. Some of the campers, especially those with children, panicked and ran across the road to hide in the sand dunes. When nothing happened except the sounding of the All Clear, they came back, ate their lunch and, quite literally, folded their tents and departed.

Life for all changed forever on that day. The newspapers and radio were full of stories about children being evacuated from danger zones and at that time we, just across the North Sea from Germany, appeared vulnerable.

There were no evacuation plans for the Blyth area but children had to be protected against air raids and that meant shelters were needed. As no bricks appeared available there was no school until the shelters were erected but we did not avoid study. At Blyth Grammar School each child was given a weekly appointment with his or her form teacher to collect homework on a multitude of subjects and return it completed the following week.

After the turn of the year in 1940 the shelters were built and we returned to school. However on our doorstep things were happening and the land and buildings in the Harbour and Wellesley Nautical School were taken over by the Royal Navy as HMS Elfin to become the second biggest land submarine station in the United Kingdom. Several hundred sailors were based in the town throughout the war.

My father obtained a contract for the supply of vegetables to the base which proved a very big job. He was allowed one full time employee but there were also several people, many retired amateur gardeners, who did a few hours work every week. Each morning father loaded the van, delivered the vegetables and collected the orders for the next day.

Dad happened to be in the harbour when a sub entered flying the Skull and Crossbones. That meant an important "kill" and an immediate celebration. Out came the rum and he, a virtual teetotaller, was included in the festivities. He was never able to say what happened next but we gathered the lads put him on the cart, turned the horse and walloped it on the rump. My mother, concerned at his long absence, went to the back door to find the horse gently grazing while Dad slept peacefully on the cart.

Entrance to the Wellesley Nautical School during the war when it was used as part of the submarine base.

The Reindeer from Norway

While on a mission to Russia the crew of the submarine Trident were presented with a young reindeer by a Russian admiral after a drunken night on vodka and brought it back to Blyth. It was tethered on the football pitch at the Wellesley base. Alan and I, on the strength of Dad's security pass, were allowed to go and see it. Apparently it killed several dogs who got too close to its hooves. We were later told it was going to a zoo and indeed it ended in Regents Park Zoo in London where it apparently lived for five years.

Each submarine did its own catering accounts, which I wrote out for my Dad, to be presented to the individual messing officers. The exceptions were when my father told me to "address this one to the Admiralty". I knew, sadly, what that meant. The boat was lost.

The RAF was also a visible presence in the South Harbour with two or three very fast motor boats designed to rescue downed RAF crew from the sea. So far as I know they never were called upon to assist airmen in our area but they did yeoman service in helping sailors in trouble.

The Germans had developed magnetic mines which were dropped by parachute into shipping lanes. Blyth bay, near to Germany, was an ideal target, as the planes could come close enough without being in danger from anti-aircraft fire.

In the terrible winter of 1940/41 eighteen ships went down in fourteen days. The explosions were horrendous. If it was daylight we rushed to the upstairs windows to see those brave small RAF boats almost flying to the scene of the disaster. Sadly there was often only debris and bodies to pick up. On one occasion father was present when a boat came in with a terribly scalded cook. He was injured when his galley blew apart and he was thrown into the sea. He died before reaching hospital.

Invasion was perceived as a very great threat on the North East coast in the latter half of 1940 and the following year which meant the Pioneer Corps descended on the area in force. They built dozens of accommodation huts with cookhouses, latrines and drains. One of their first activities was the securing and refurbishing of the gun emplacements built on the Links during the First World War.

Slightly inland from the guns were ancillary buildings. Someone had the idea they should be camouflaged as bijou residences! They were given chimney pots, domestic doors and window frames were painted on the three sides visible from the land and one even had a trellis with roses.

I have no recollection of the installation of the guns but we certainly knew, though never why, they were fired. They made a tremendous noise and the vibration was responsible for some of the windows we lost.

We got so used to unidentified explosions that we often assumed that an animal had triggered off a mine in the dunes. On at least one occasion we were wrong. It was a sunny afternoon and six sailors signed out from the base saying they were going for a walk. They didn't return and were posted AWOL (Absent Without Leave). Their homes were searched and for some time watched.

The camp site before the Second World War

After the war when mines were being cleared in the dunes human bones, enough to make six skeletons, were found. I still think of the poor families of those lads and the shame and humiliation they must have suffered.

Armed Sentry

There was always an armed sentry just outside Link House which we had to pass to get home. There was no problem during the daytime as a kid in school uniform could hardly be mistaken for the vanguard of the German Army.

But once it was dark the challenge "Who goes there?" was no joke and had to be answered promptly and correctly. It was drummed into us by our parents that answering "Donald Duck" was not funny in the pitch dark when faced with a jittery man with a loaded rifle!

It obviously never occurred to our parents that we were at any other risk. Surrounded as we were by so many strangers, lonely young men, we were never in any danger of molestation.

During the war, depending on weather and wind conditions, squadrons of German bombers came over the coast anywhere between the Borders and Yorkshire (Blyth at War Part Two page 64). Initially we always asked were they "ours" or "theirs" but even children soon learnt the difference in engine sounds.

Often, before the Alert sounded our guns opened up and the search lights made the sky light as day. Then it was over and we got to sleep only to have a repeat performance three or four hours later as the bombers headed home.

Almost from day one the Royal Navy, by far the biggest of the three forces, had organised social activities on the base. The Army and RAF provided bed and board and training for the men but there was a lot of time when they had nothing to do for even Blyth was out of bounds on occasions.

My mother decided to do something and decided to turn a cottage next door to our house into a canteen. Friends provided tableware, cutlery, floor rugs, armchairs, card tables, games and a lot of books. To my delight the piano was moved next door – no more hated practice!

Good Bakers

Friends of mother, like her, good bakers, produced scones, pies and sausage rolls on an almost conveyor belt basis as rationing had not started in the early days.

It was an instant hit with standing room only. One bedroom was for cards, a second bedroom was a "quiet" room, although the noise from the downstairs living room was deafening. Mother and her helpers had to join the WVS in order to run it and as a result received parcels of home knitted khaki and Air Force blue socks, scarves and balaclava helmets to be distributed at their discretion. Touchingly some of the parcels contained a tablet of soap, sweets or even a ten shilling note – fifty pence nowadays.

The canteen was open afternoon and evening, 365 days a year for the next four years. Its demise came in 1944 when the troops withdrew to head south in preparation for the D-Day landings. The furniture in the canteen, including the piano, now in a sad state, was carried outside and chopped up for firewood. Nothing was wasted in those days.

Around that time there were only enough troops to keep the links and the beach secure. This was as much for the safety of the civilian population as for any other reason as the whole area was still very dangerous.

Life had been hard and sometime frightening during wartime but great friendships were cemented and there was much humour and kindness. As a family we were extremely fortunate to suffer nothing worse than a few broken windows. If it had not been for the terrible toll of death and maiming one could say it was an experience worth having lived through.

Link House before the First World War now standing derelict with rumours the site will become an hotel.

The Big Storm

The most ferocious storm ever to hit the town of Blyth occurred on Friday, October the 26th, 1900. It started mid-afternoon and lasted until dawn the following day causing one death and chaos to industry, shops and families.

The storm began with heavy rain and sleet driven by a strong North West wind. Most of the people stayed indoors in front of fires and when they opened their curtains after it abated were astonished to find the damage it had caused. As reported by the Blyth News: "The sight must have caused a lot of people to vigorously rub their eyes and ask themselves twice over whether they were dreaming or not."

The streets, it was reported, had disappeared under a "surging sea" which lapped high against shop windows and houses. A deep and continuous river ran up Waterloo Road, past the railway station and along Turner Street. The Blyth News reported the appearance was as though the sea had risen and swept over the whole town. It had become an "Anglicised Venice" isolating the Waterloo district from Cowpen Quay. The railway bridge across Turner Street was the only access between the two districts.

The Waterloo Supply Stores in Havelock Street were badly hit by the floods. The store is now the Celebrations Gift and Card shop.

Folly Road, now known as Park Road, was the lowest lying area of the town and was the most seriously affected. Only the tip of the iron garden railings showed and the water in the front rooms of some of the houses reached as high as the keyboards of pianos.

The centre of Blyth was particularly hit by the floods as can be seen in this picture taken in Waterloo Road. This area was to be badly hit by fire in 1904 which led to some extensive rebuilding of the Thompson's Arcade.

The nearby Crofton Mill pit was put out of action as the water swamped the fires of the engine house halting the cages. Fortunately few miners were at work as it was the eve of "Pay Saturday" when the miners received their fortnightly wages.
It was also the day when housewives stocked up with food but the money was of no use as the shops were shut because of the flooding.

A crowd assembled in the Market Place which included the shop assistants who were temporarily out of work. There they were entertained by a man trying to swim up Turner Street.

It was impossible to walk in most parts of the town and indeed two rowing boats were used to carry people from their homes in Folly Road while Newsham did not escape the flood as the Newsham railway station was filled to the roof.

Only one death was reported, that of James Yellowly, the owner of a pony and trap who had been ferrying people around Newsham. He was missed at about half past eight in the evening and after a two hour search was found to be drowned. His death, however, remained a mystery.

Little Change

By noon on Saturday there was little change although the crowds turned out that night to the Theatre Royal, which had been partly flooded, to see Captain Pomeroy Gilbert's company from the Princess Theatre in London a play entitled "The Still Alarm".

Incidentally, before the theatre closed in 1965, the boiler room under the stage was still susceptible to flooding, so much so that the fires could only be stoked by someone wearing thigh boots.

The flood slowly subsided on the Sunday when the damage was assessed. The storm cost businesses thousands of pounds. Hedley & Company, drapers, lost £300; Two grocers, Mr. Taylor of Cowpen Quay and Mr. Straker of Havelock Street were down £200; Joseph Lee, a Turner Street draper, lost the same amount while A.A. Askwith, a supplier of hats from his Turner Street shop, and Bon Marche lost £100.

The first fire engine in Blyth, which had been delivered only a few months before, was called in action almost round the clock to pump water from the cellars of public houses while Sunday services were held after the water was cleared from St. Mary's Church.

Regent Street from the ferry end some months after the floods cut Cowpen Quay off the rest of Blyth.

After the big storm subsided the horse drawn fire fighting unit, the only one in Blyth, pictured here outside its headquarters in Seaforth Street, was in great demand to help pump out the many businesses, offices and public houses which had been flooded. It was some twenty three years later before a motorised fire engine (below) arrived in the town.

The Blyth Hero

The story of a Blyth man who took part in the sinking of the Bismark, helped rescue two trapped comrades from a sinking ship and won the Distinguished Service Medal only to die in Tobruk can now be told.

The name of Allen Glen Branley is one of the names of more than 200 Blyth men who died in the Second World War inscribed on the War Memorial in Ridley Park in the town. But he is the only one with a DSM alongside his name.

Allen Branley was the son of Thomas and Janet Branley and at the outbreak of war joined the crew of the destroyer HMS Sikh and was aboard when it left South Shields after refitting. His first major contact with the enemy was in the battle of Cape Bon in the Central Mediterranean on December 13th.1941.

War records state that three British destroyers, including the Sikh, located two Italian warships by radar. Racing at 30 knots the boats were able to remain hidden against the dark until within firing distance. From a range of 1,000 yards the Sikh fired two torpedoes into the cruiser Birbiana which burst into flames from stem to stern.

A second cruiser, the Giussano, then opened fire but failed to cause any damage to the British ships before being sunk by three salvoes from the Sikh and a torpedo from HMS Legion.

HMS Sikh.

It was for this action that Allen Branley, was awarded the Distinguished Service Medal – second only to the Victoria Cross – but the full details of his bravery are not revealed although he is believed to have been in the torpedo crew.
In the citation from King George V1 it states he showed, coolness, skill and enterprise during the battle which led to no British casualties and the sinking of two Italian cruisers, an e-boat and serious damage to an enemy torpedo boat.

Less than a year later Allen Branley was dead. An ill fated commando raid was launched by the Allies on Benghazi in September, 1942, and the Sikh was sent in to embark the commandos. She was spotted by a shore searchlight and batteries opened fire. The boat was hit on a number of occasions so badly that HMS Zulu, which was also involved in the action, laid a smokescreen to help take the Sikh crew off. The firing was so severe the Zulu was ordered to withdraw.

The Sikh skipper, Captain St John Micklethwaite, who had given the order to abandon ship, fired the scuttling charges to stop his boat from falling into enemy hands.

Allen Branley had, in the meantime swum away from the ship, but, according to unconfirmed reports, returned to release two of his shipmates who were trapped. By the time he got back into the water it was ablaze with burning oil and he was badly burned.

Taken prisoner by the Italians, he was treated in a hospital in Tobruk but died a few days later on September 15th., 1942, at the age of 23. He was buried in the War Cemetery in Tobruk leaving a wife, Mary, living in Blyth, who had recently given birth to a baby boy, who was also named Allen.

Memories of Allen Branley were recalled in 2009 when a lady called at the Central Methodist Church in Blyth and handed over a metal plaque carrying the name of the seaman and two others who had died in the war. It had been fixed to the Lords Table in the now demolished Zion Methodist Church. While the table was being moved to the Annitsford Methodist Church the plaque fell off into the road and was run over by the wheels of the truck.

It was found by the Annitsford lady who, not knowing the story, kept it for many years until handing it over to the Central Methodist Church.

A.G. Branley's Grave in Tripoli.

Detective work by retired Blyth schoolteacher George Robson uncovered the story and the posthumous award of the DSM to Allen Branley.

He recalled: "Apparently a few days before his death Mary Branley, who only had one arm, had given birth to a baby boy. She sent a photograph of the baby and Allen was so distressed to see the boy only had one arm. It was later to transpire that the baby had two arms – it was just the way the picture had been taken.

"Allen junior moved to Scotland but 30 years later returned to Blyth to attend the funeral of a friend who was shown an article I had written in the Blyth News about his father and the plaque. After the funeral he traced me to the United Reformed Church where I was playing the organ at a wedding and we linked up with another of his old friends, George Watson, when we had a good chinwag."

Allen Jnr. was given the plaque to take home to Edinburgh but he and the two other fallen are commemorated in the Central Methodist Church on a new plaque which was made to be displayed on the church font.

Allen Branley jnr. died in 2011 at the age of 68.

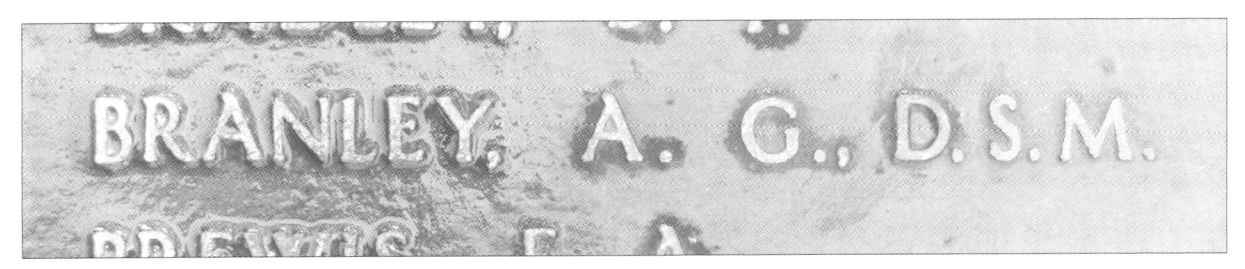

Memorial Plaque at Blyth Memorial.

The End of Blyth Grammar School

A building in which thousands of the brightest youngsters from Blyth and its surrounding villages fell to the demolition machines in 2011, bringing to an end the last contact with Secondary and Grammar schools in the town.

Education for bright youngsters was introduced to Blyth through the Higher Grade School in Beaconsfield Street, which opened in 1890. On its closure in 1913, pupils were transferred to the new Secondary School in Plessey Road. This became the Blyth Grammar School in 1944 and continued educating the brighter pupils until 1965 when a High School at Cowpen was opened. The building, however, did not stand empty for long as it was taken over by New Delaval Middle School. This tenancy lasted until 2010 when it closed, with the introduction of the two tier education system by Northumberland County Council.

One man who remembers the switch from Secondary to Grammar school is 82-yearold Kenneth Reah, now in retirement in Sheffield. He was born at 44, Seventh Avenue, Blyth, on December the 10th. 1929, to John and Ethel Reah. He was the younger son in a family of two boys and a girl. Just before the war, the family moved to Union Street, opposite the fire station.

On leaving school, Ken went to Kings College, Newcastle, to gain a B.A. Fine Art. He returned there after two years National Service in the R.A.F., to take a Diploma in Education. After some years teaching in Sussex, he was appointed Lecturer in Art and Craft at Darlington Teacher Training College, (later Darlington College of Education).

Ken Reah.

On being made redundant in 1978, when the college was closed, along with many others, by the government, he moved to Sheffield to do an M.A. in English Language, following this with a Ph.D. Thereafter, he taught English Language and Linguistics at the University of Sheffield until retirement. He still lives in Sheffield with his wife, the crime writer, Danuta Reah, where he paints, makes sculpture and writes. These are his memories.

Cane Discipline

School for me began at Crofton Junior where discipline of the cane was administered by the headmaster, Mr. Redford. What a difference when on my arrival at the Secondary School, later to be named the Grammar School, I really felt I had been transported into one of those school stories I used to read so avidly. There were masters and mistresses who wore gowns, prefects and "prep" and there were four houses each with a housemaster and housemistresses.

There were important differences though. The schools in the stories were never co-educational and in them discipline was maintained by corporal punishment, just as it was at Crofton Junior. What heinous misdemeanours could justify a big man assaulting an eight-year-old with a stick? But there was no corporal punishment in our new school although it was widely believed there was a cane in the cupboard in the headmaster's study.

I began the secondary school in September, 1941, having some time earlier passed the eleven-plus, known as "the scholarship". It would not be true to say I was surprised to see my name on the pass list in the Blyth News the day the results were published, since I had spent the last year in the Crofton Junior "scholarship class" where we received a lot of exam practice. Up to that point my education had cost nothing. Of course it was free at the secondary school but there were expenses to be met which could place a strain on family finances.

In the junior school P.T. in the school yard was 20 minutes of arms stretch, knees bend, in four lines conducted by the class teacher in his pullover. The secondary school had a gym, which also served as the assembly hall, with vaulting horses, boxes, wall bars and ropes. Miss Watkins, the teacher who took us, required us to have gym vests, shorts and gym shoes which we had to change into when it became known as P.E. (physical education) instead of P.T. We also needed football boots and stockings and a woodwork apron. There were also sundries, pens, pencils, set squares, protractors and a box or case to hold them.

Then there was the school uniform, a requirement not too strictly applied due to the austerity existing in wartime. But what first form boy would not want to wear with pride the navy blue and maroon cap with its badge bearing the motto "Tenax et Fidelis" (True and Faithful). The final touch was the leather satchel, haversack-style, for the books and daily homework.

There was also an unwritten tradition that passing the scholarship got you a new bike, if your parents could afford it. Mine could not.

Terms at the secondary school, after the six weeks summer holiday, started a week after other schools in the town giving us the opportunity of gloating through the railings of the junior school. We looked forward to the first day with excitement and trepidation because of the rumours of initiation rituals. These mostly involved immersion in water, quite like a baptism and did happen but they were firmly banned some years later when Mr. Parslow took over the headship.

So that day in the late summer of 1941 sixty new faces passed through the school gates, boys and girls, for the building was co-educational like our junior school, although most grammar schools at the time were single sex.

Though the sexes mixed in classrooms there was a form of segregation in that boys and girls went in through separate gates – the west and the east – into their own yards with their own changing rooms and toilets.

Blyth Grammar School.

One of the wonders for me was the huge expanse of playing field behind the school building. There was no playing field at Crofton nor indeed, I believe, at other senior schools except St. Wilfrids.

We were divided into two forms – One North and One South – which caused me to be separated from my best friend, Rex Hitchfield, and my cousin, Joan Carlisle.
Our form teacher in One South was Miss Urma Crisp, who came from the family which kept the light on St. Mary's Island. She lived at Seaton Sluice and talked rather posh. She taught us French, our first experience of a foreign language, and she must have been good because now, at 83, I remember everything she taught us. The headmaster, Nigel Parry, gave us our initiation into the more exacting intricacies of Latin.

The education we were offered was entirely conventional with much talk, lecturing, note-taking and rote learning – everything consolidated by homework and tested by exams. Mr. Herbert Hall, in the workshop beyond the boys yard, gave us the skills in handling tools and measuring which, over the years, I have always been grateful for. Phyllis Hough took us for art and it was she who set me en route to art school and a career as an artist and academic.

Blyth Grammar School, Third Form South, 1952. Back Row: Tom Miles, Jackie Day, Gordon Patterson, Brian Turnbull. Middle row: Marie Forsythe, Ronnie Carr, Peter Hawks, Mike Henzell, Ken Davey, Wilf Carr, Diane Shewan, Anne McPherson. Front Row: Annie Ratter, Edna Mitcheson, Margaret Urwin, Gerald Smith (Form Prefect), Miss Una Chrisp (form teacher), Margaret Irwin, Maureen Wilby, Betty Potts, Irene Holloway.

At the end of the second year the two forms now became East and West and in 3E we had to choose the academic path and continue with Latin or 3W for woodwork, domestic and horticultural science. These were momentous choices which determined which school certificate subjects we would take which, in turn, had an important bearing on our future careers.

The 1944 Education Act completely restructured secondary education introducing the Thirteen Plus test, which offered another chance to those who had just missed the Eleven Plus, and turning secondary schools, including Blyth, into grammar schools. And in order to counter the gender imbalance in the 1944 intake an all girls form was created which led to a general increase in civilised behaviour and an injection of new life into the school. We could now boast a splendid girls choir. I don't know why we weren't invited as we sang lustily in our weekly segregated half hour of music taken by Mr. Alfie Campbell.

The cleared Grammar School site with the new owners, the Bede Academy building in the distant background.

The thirteen plus test led to an influx of new pupils into the middle of school, their class designated the Remove – shades of Greyfriars – and a need for further accommodation. A range of wooden buildings in Barras Avenue were taken over as extra classrooms and were known as the JIC – the Juvenile Instruction Centre. Much to our delight space was found there for a small common room for the exclusive use of the Lower Sixth form.

Now the war in Europe was over without us once having to use the brick built air raid shelters on the edge of Plessey Road. We escaped fighting for our King and Country but we remembered the prefects who smiled benignly down on us first formers and who got through their school certificate and higher exams and left to be immediately conscripted into the armed forces.

Some came back to visit the old school on speech day wearing army, navy or air force uniforms but some, sadly never came back.

The notice informing the public the site was to be playing grounds for the academy. Shortly after the takeover two sets of rugby posts were erected.

The Blyth Squatters Battle

A grandmother burst into a room in a house in Newbiggin and shouted to her daughter: "Quick, get packed there's some huts empty at Blyth." And that was the start of an illegal invasion which saw empty army barracks along the Links and at Cambois being taken over by families shortly after the Second World War.

The grandmother was Mrs. Annie Jackson and she was fed up living in extremely crowded conditions in the seaside town. Within minutes she, her three young sons, her married daughter, Ellen Bower, and her two young children had packed their belongings and set off for Blyth. They arrived in time to commandeer two of the seventeen huts which had been used by the soldiers operating the battery protecting the harbour and town. The empty huts in and around Blyth Links caused a furore in the town as servicemen returned from the war to find an acute shortage of housing and no help being offered by the local authority.

The first intimation that trouble was brewing over the huts came in July, 1946, when the homeless ex-servicemen and their families threatened to take them over following the lead of squatters at Army camps in Scunthorpe, Sheffield and Chesterfield.

It was reported at the time they were contemplating the action "spurred on by fruitless efforts to obtain somewhere to live and the unsympathetic attitude of landladies and officials."

They wanted to know why the buildings were being allowed to become derelict and dilapidated through months of non-habitation instead of the huts being converted into homes. A deputation of ex-servicemen, some living in overcrowded houses and others who had failed to find permanent rooms or lodgings, urged Blyth Council to convert the hutments into habitable homes.

A view of the huts.

One Dunkirk veteran, now working as a builders labourer who had four young children, was the spokesmen for the ex-servicemen. He said: "We should be given some priority as a reward for our sacrifices. If steps are not taken soon we are going to take the law into our own hands and move in."

But a word of warning was issued at the time by Captain Cyril Shewan, chairman of the Blyth branch of the British Legion. He said: "If the men carry out the threat they would only have squatters rights. These huts will have to have considerable work done upon them to make them habitable. They do not have cooking facilities in individual huts and only communal sanitary arrangements."

But his warning fell on deaf ears and it was not the army veterans who started the squatters rush. It was a 22-year-old shipyard worker, Mr. John Armstrong, who began it in Blyth by taking over one of the Gloucester Lodge huts with his wife and young son. They had been living in overcrowded conditions with in-laws in Bowes Street. The hut they took over had a living room, brick fireplace and two bedrooms. They had no gas or electricity and lighting was provided by candles or lamps. Their lavatory was in a nearby wooden block which also had washing facilities.

On the day the Armstrongs moved squatters commandeered an empty military camp at Wembley near Cambois as Bedlington Council was also facing a squatters rebellion over housing shortages.

Eighteen families took over the 30 Nissen huts by chalking their names on the doors or marking them "Taken". The new tenants cut down barbed wire fences to allow carts and lorries to drive into the camp to unload furniture.

In Blyth the second family moving to Gloucester Lodge was the Broadley's. John Broadley was 56, a veteran of both world wars, and had a wife, three sons and three daughters who were aged from ten to 23.

As news of the squatting spread through Blyth other families, servicemen and locals, moved in and within a few days all the huts were taken or reserved. One hut was occupied by Mrs. Jean King, a mother of two, whose husband, a Dunkirk veteran, was a former Northumberland Fusilier. She said at the time: "At long last I am happy in a little home of my own. We were living in another woman's house and I am grateful to them for sharing their home with us. Actually last Sunday they cooked a dinner for us and sent it along,

"I have furnished the house and laid down my Utility lino bought with my ration units and put up my pink muslin curtains. There is a play corner for my daughter and she has just spent the whole morning on the beach and brought home sea shells she's gathered. I love it here."

But for Mrs. James Taylor, the wife of a miner who lived in No. 10 Battery Drive, life was not so happy as their free coal was stopped by the colliery owners. Cowpen Coal Company claimed only those who paid rent qualified for the concession as did the Hartley Main Collieries.

The Taylor family was just one of several miner squatters affected. Mrs James said: "We all pay five shillings a week into a pool but this is not

Moving into the huts.

regarded as rent. We are hoping the problem will be resolved before the winter sets in." In order to get coal for their stoves many families scavenged for the fuel on the spoil heaps at New Delaval and New Hartley.

While there was sympathy in the town for the situation of the squatters there was also resentment by hundreds on the council housing list. They feared, wrongly as it turned out, the squatters would get priority on the list.

The Mayor and Mayoress of Blyth , Alderman and Mrs. Aaron Walton later paid a visit to the camp and told the squatters if they had been in the same position they would have followed their example rather than live in the cramped housing conditions they had been enduring.

Mr. and Mrs. Tom Wyatt were another Blyth couple who moved to Gloucester Lodge. Their daughter, Mrs. Moira Douglass now 74 and living in Monkdale, Cowpen, was seven when they took over one of the corrugated iron roofed huts.

"There were none of the posh ones, the wooden ones, left. Ours was very cold and we had to use gas cylinders," she said. "The toilets were in a brick block which had been built for the soldiers and it was very scary going along the passage in the darkness."

But Moira was in her element during the summer as she had the job of walking the beach ponies and taking the money for the "shuggy boats" situated on the sand below the promenade. "I didn't get paid very much, less than two bob, but I enjoyed it."

Four years later Moira and her family moved from Gloucester Lodge to a hut near the Wellesley Nautical School and after two years moved into a new house on the Cowpen Estate.

There was a certain stigma if you were a squatter as a young man, embarrassed at living there, found when walking a girl on the links. He had not told her he lived in the huts but as they were passing one his brothers poked his head out and shouted: "Hey Jimmy, your tea's ready."

"Shuggy Boats" - the swings were a feature of Blyth beachfor over 100 years and were well used by the squatters families. Alas the swings, and the popular pony rides, have long gone.

Battery Drive

Among the early arrivals at the Gloucester Lodge camp was Mrs. Annie Jackson, her second husband, Tom Coates, her three sons Matty, Jim and Raymond Jackson, her daughter Mrs. Ellen Bowen, and her two young sons, Ron and Matty Bowen. The families took over two huts which were later to be known as 2 and 8 Battery Drive.

For Ron Bowen, now a 69 year old retired miner, living in Cowpen Estate, No. 2 hut became his home for the next nine years.

He recalls: "Our hut had two bedrooms and another room with a Donkey Stove in the centre with a metal chimney poking out through the roof. Some families put up partitions to give them an extra bedroom but none of us had running water or toilets.

"There were two stand pipes at each end of the camp and it was we youngsters who had to go daily to fetch the water. The toilets were two privees in the only army washhouse."

What Ron did not know was that his future wife, Jane, was living on the camp. They met up some 15 years later at Plessey Road school and celebrated their golden wedding this year.

Jane, who's 67, says her memories of the camp were sharing her bed with her three sisters and the

Ron and Jane Bowen.

earwigs, known as forkytails. "They were everywhere, crawling over you as you slept and it was so cold our parents would take the proggy mat carpets off the floor to put over us in bed." The cooking, she said, was done on the top of the stove. Number eight was to be Jane's home for eight years before her family was given a council house in Twelfth Avenue.

19

Ron remembers one incident with humour. Being an ex-army camp, pieces of equipment were lying around and one teenager found some wet cartridge shells. He decided to dry them off by standing them on the top of the donkey stove.

"When they exploded they shot off through the roof, fortunately for him," he said.

The squatters rebellion though resulted in the military authorities releasing the huts to Blyth council four months after the takeovers. Improvements were then made to the buildings and tenants, because they were now paying rents, got places on the council housing list.

Inside the huts.

As families moved out on being rehoused others moved in, one set of newcomers being the Hutchings family. It was a move seven year old Brian Hutchings did not object too. He spent the next eight years living in No. 7 Battery Drive less than a stones throw from the beach, and the concrete ship with steering wheel close to the Jubilee Café. Their hut was equipped with a coal fired stove stoked by fuel from his miner father's coal allowance.

By the time they moved in the wooden huts all had electricity installed by Billy Wells, who owned a garage across from the squatters, who took pity on the conditions the squatters were living under

Brian, now living in retirement in Cornwall, said: "We were eventually moved by the council to a house in Sycamore Avenue and while it was nice to have a proper house a youngster could not ask for a better place to live, particularly during the summer."

Ron, Matty and Toby the dog in the Dunes.

While the majority of squatters were decent families some of them proved not to be of the nicest type as a Blyth Council rent collector at the time can vouch. The official, who asked not to be named, said: "The rent was only five shillings a week but some of them refused to pay.

"As one tenant told me: 'You are just in it for the commission you get.' I pointed out to him if I was I would not make a living from them as they weren't paying anything.

"Unfortunately these tenants could not be evicted as it meant the council legally had to find them other accommodation."

But he added: "I felt sorry for the other families and the conditions they were having to live in and I think we were all pleased when the last squatter left in 1962."

Ron Bowen, featured in this article, sadly passed away before publication. I shall remember him as an interesting, warmhearted, welcoming man.

Jim Harland

The Phoenix – The Last Theatre In Town

One thousand five hundred youngsters trained for the stage; the Church v Phoenix "no drinks or gambling" dispute; the two strange ghostly happenings which frightened members and the stars wanting to appear in Blyth, just part of the intriguing Blyth Phoenix Theatre story.

The first recorded public performances of plays in Blyth took place at the Ridley Arms Hotel in the summer of 1815 but it was not until 60 years later the first theatre, the Octagon Music Hall, opened in 1874.

Since then the town has had three Theatre Royals, 1875, 1888 and 1900, the Granthams Assembly Rooms, 1899, the Hippodrome, 1902, the Gaiety Theatre of Varieties, 1906, and the Empire Electric Palace, 1911. Keeping the flag flying as the last theatre in town is the Phoenix in Beaconsfield Street. This is how it came into being.

In 1964 the Blyth Arts Council was formed by a number of public spirited citizens under the chairmanship of Alex Haxon. They met in the upstairs hall of the Blyth Labour Rooms in Waterloo Road, now the Flying Horse public house, to promote the arts in the town. Within a year Blyth had lost its only theatre, the Theatre Royal in Trotter Street, when it closed permanently.

The closure of the Methodist Church in Beaconsfield Street threw it a lifeline and the Arts Council, with the aid of grants and money raising ventures, took it over. Unfortunately, written into the sales agreement by the church authorities was a covenant that no alcohol and gambling could take place in the building.

David Garrett, the present theatre director, who was involved in the early days of the takeover, said: "This immediately stopped any money-making activities needed to keep the theatre afloat. It hit lettings on the head. Indeed local organisations, such as the Women's Guild who used it weren't able to have a raffle for cakes and suchlike to raise the money to pay the rental for use of the building."

David, a retired schoolteacher, said when the takeover was completed all that remained in the

David Garrett outside the theatre.

church were the wooden pews. A platform had to be installed as a stage while the pews were replaced with second hand seats obtained from bingo halls and cinemas.

The Arts Council had, in the meantime, learned that the Phoenix Drama Group, which had performed in the Cowpen and Crofton Welfare Hall but had gone out of existence, had a theatre building fund containing £600 which was now languishing in a bank. The Arts Council learned the money could be released if the new theatre was called the Phoenix. When it was agreed there was no legal hindrance in taking over the cash.

There certainly was, however, in the 70's when the Arts Council, now the Blyth Arts and Community Association found itself involved in a legal fight which threatened to be heard in the High Court.

It concerned moves by the Arts Council to open a bar in the building. John Ryman, QC, who was also M.P. for Blyth, represented the Council and just when it looked as though the dispute was London bound the church authorities withdrew their objection. They had been advised they were unlikely to win as the building was now a "change of useage." And so an alcoholic and coffee bar was installed in an area between the church and the hall.

The theatre though was working at a disadvantage with a poor stage and lack of the usual stage facilities. In the early 1970's all things changed when contributions from trusts and charitable bodies brought in £5,000 which enabled a proper stage with lights and stage equipment to be installed. Local efforts were also made to raise cash and these included a week long production of the Sound of Music at the Wallaw Cinema by the Blyth Valley Operatics – formed for just the one show. Singers, actors and back stage staff were drawn from societies in and around the region.

This resulted in a cheque for £500 being presented to the Arts Council on the last night raised from the record 8,221 people who saw the show paying just three and four shillings a ticket.

All the money-raising efforts led to the first musical being staged in the old church – Cabaret – with Trevor Harder playing the lead role of Emcee. Years later Trevor presented the Phoenix with mementoes he had saved when the Theatre Royal auditorium was being demolished. These now hang in the bar of the new theatre.

Over the years there were two strange happenings which frightened members. The first occurred in the ladies toilet in the old church building when the ghostly figure of an old lady carrying a basket was seen. It led to girls and women refusing to use the toilet.

The second occurred in the upstairs office of the new building when Paul Worth, the treasurer and long serving member of the Phoenix, was carrying a considerable sum of money to put in the safe after a show. He was kneeling opening the safe when he became aware of the presence of a man with a tartan waistcoat standing alongside him who suddenly disappeared. .

He said: "I was so scared I threw the money in the air and raced downstairs. When others went up they found all the money scattered around the office.

"I don't believe in the supernatural but that certainly happened."

The plaques salvaged from the Theatre Royal by Trevor Harder as it was being demolished.

Some members swear the two figures were those of members who had recently passed away.

It was in the late 1980's when disaster brought the theatre to a halt. The roof of the building started sagging and had to be closed because of the danger to the public. Investigations revealed a design fault in the timbers when it was built some 80 years earlier.

The Phoenix Theatre was moved into the adjacent church hall, which became known as The Studio, while discussions about the future were held.

One scheme that was considered was for the Phoenix to take over the empty Drill Hall on the Quayside, owned by Fergusons Transport and plans were drawn incorporating a theatre and restaurant which could cost up to £750,000.

David Garrett said: "Lack of money and support by Blyth Council led to the scheme being scrapped and it was decided to try and find a solution to our present premises." A buildings expert came up with the idea that the church roof could be saved but at a cost and it was then they were advised to build a new theatre on the site. Plans were drawn up and an application was drafted in double quick time for a grant from the National Lottery which had been running for just a year.

The application was successful and the theatre was given a grant of £780,000. With financial support from the Foundation for Sport and Recreation plus a five figure sum the Phoenix had in the bank the new theatre was built in twelve months at a cost of £1,250,000.

The honour of starting the demolition of the old building fell to three year old Robbie Love the youngest member of the Phoenix. Unfortunately, despite much cajoling by the photographers, he was in a non-smiling mood the whole of the ceremony as can be seen by the accompanying picture.

Robbie though retained his interest in the theatre and in 2013 took the male lead in the Lancaster University production of Cabaret.

In June 1997 HRH Princess Margaret visited the theatre and in September of the same year it was officially opened by Matthew Ridley, the present Viscount Ridley of Blagdon,

By this time the Phoenix had become the premier theatrical venue in the town with an annual pantomime making the major financial contribution to the running of the theatre. The Phoenix also enhanced its reputation by becoming the first society in the North East to perform the hit musicals Little Voice, Whistle Down the Wind and Cats.

The Young Phoenix group can rightly claim to have introduced more than 1,400 youngsters to the stage since its foundation in 1978. Some of the "graduates" have gone on to join the professional ranks such as Phillip Correia and Ivan Wilkinson.

Robbie Love, the youngest member of the Phoenix at three, starts the demolition.

But David Garrett says: "Regrettably we lose most of the youngsters when they reach 15 or 16 because of school exams and the like but nevertheless we have a long waiting list for a one of the 40 places. What is very rewarding to us is that we are being recognized as a good venue whereas in the past we've contacted agents for professional acts we now find they are ringing us."

Among the "names" to have appeared at the Phoenix are Barry Cryer, Ned Sherrin, Alvin Stardust, operatic trio Blake and Nicholas Parsons.

In the Phoenix archives lie plans for even further development of the site which would result in the heightening of the church hall and digging down to improve access to the stage area.

As David says: "Now, if someone was to win the Euro lottery and make a healthy donation we might just get the job done."

The Phoenix Theatre exterior.

Memories of the Shipyard

Workers summoned to their jobs by boys on bicycles; a mans world invaded by women, the power of the unions and a shipbuilder building houses, part of the fascinating history of Blyth Shipyard.

Shipbuilding on the River Blyth was started in 1750 by Edmund Hannay, a Scottish shipwright, at a small yard near the Customs House. Forty years later there were three producing vessels alongside rope, sail, block and tackle makers.

There was shipbuilding at Seaton Sluice around that time which produced several vessels but the industry had vanished by the turn of the century.

Around the time of the Battle of Trafalgar, in which two local men, William Murton and Robert Nicholson, fought on HMS Victory and HMS Bellerophan, the number of boat builders in Blyth had risen to six. Shipbuilding facilities in the port were vastly improved in 1811 with the building of a dock by Stoveld and Company.

Ships made of wood continued to be built until 1874 when the industrial revolution led to ships being constructed from iron. Initially this had a detrimental effect on Blyth because the river was too shallow for them. This led to the halving of the coal trade from Blyth in eight years to 181,000 tons.

Trade though began to pick up with the deepening of the river which allowed ships of up to 1,000 tons to enter. It also led to building being started on the first iron ship by Chapman, Towers and Horn. It was never completed but Hodgson and Soulsby had more success when they launched the 1,000 ton Speedwell fitted with a 99 horse power steam engine.

Shipbuilding progressed rapidly from that time and in 1914 the Admiralty had a merchantman being built at Blyth converted into an aircraft carrier, the Ark Royal, the first of its kind in the Royal Navy.

There was a serious falling off of work after the war and the Cowpen Dry Docks and Shipbuilding Co. Ltd., took over Ritsons Shipbuilding Company near Bates Pit and in 1932 changed its name to the Blyth Dry Docks and Shipbuilding Company Ltd.

Launch of King Theseus in 1960.

The new company was finding work hard to get until the emergence of Hitler led to a change in fortunes and a boom in shipbuilding.

In 1944 the Mollers Trust of Hong Kong took over the company but as had happened after the end of the First World War had little success in securing orders in the post war era. In 1947 alone nine orders were cancelled and over the next 20 years records show other orders were abandoned. It was in 1966 the town was shocked, and over a thousand men immediately thrown out of work, when the Moller Brothers called in the receivers without warning.

Despite a hunt for others to take over the yard all attempts failed bringing to an end 265 years of shipbuilding history during which 380 vessels were built, overhauled or repaired.

One of the men thrown out of work that summer of 1966 was Joe Mann, now 87, the son of Charles and Marie Mann of Hamilton Street. His father, a miner, did not want his son to follow him into the pits. Joe subsequently left Forster Senior School at the age of 14 on a Tuesday and started work in the shipyard as an apprentice rivet catcher the next day.

He worked a five and a half day week for ten shillings which was dutifully handed over to his mother. But he was not without money. Every Saturday morning he turned up at the Duke of Wellington Club where he was handed two shillings from the riveters who met there every week to share out their piecework earnings.

Joe narrowly escaped being conscripted to fight in the war as he had just started as an apprentice plater. This put him in a reserved occupation category but his best pal, Tom Charlton, was not so lucky. He was just about to sign his indentures on reaching 16 but was called into the army. On his return to civilian life he had to start his apprenticeship at the age of 22!

During the war single girls were conscripted into the three forces having a choice of joining the ATS, Wrens or WAAF. One Blyth girl now 90, too bashful to be identified, was called up and after training in factories in Wallsend and Liverpool found herself one of over 30 women recruited to work in the Blyth yard.

Joe Mann.

"I spent two years putting holes in sheets of metal with a steam hammer," she said. "It was boring work although my five workmates, all men, treated me very well. I was pleased to get rid of my work clothes and put my uniform back on."

For the next two years she worked as a clerk in depots around Britain before being posted to Germany from where she was demobbed.

Joe remembers when the women came to the yard in 1942 to help overcome a manpower shortage. "It was rather strange to see women in what had been solely a mans world," he said. "They were trained as fitters, welders and blacksmiths. I can remember one, a pretty lass who worked the big steam hammer.

"They had their own what was called a 'rest room'. It was a brick extension built on top of another building at the north end of the yard just behind Thompson's Red Stamp Store on Regent Street. If any of the lasses were working at the other end of the yard they had a long trek for relief."

For a time the yard diverted into building three storeyed prefabricated flats for Blyth Council which proved highly successful and popular. Several were erected on Cowpen Road and lasted some 20 years before their steel skeletons were used to update them with bricks and mortar.

Joe Mann in working clothes.

The prefabricated houses built by the shipyard on Cowpen Road lasted several years before Blyth Council moved out the tenants for a year then used the steel frame of the buildings to build the new ones around.

The flats today with several obscured by a belt of trees

In order to keep the yard going the yard also branched out into producing steelwork for major projects such as the Sutton Road Bridge, the Northumberland Fire Service headquarters at Morpeth, Blyth Grammar School gymnasium, a 200 ton crane at Lowestoft and the replacement railway bridge over the river at Bebside.

But the additional work failed to halt the closure of the yard in 1966. It was not the first time, however, Joe Mann had been thrown out of work and put on the dole.

He recalls: "It happened on a number of occasions when we were laid off during the poor times at the Yard. Once it lasted so long I spent six months as a binman for the council."

After 1966 Joe worked at Swan Hunters on the Tyne and then again for Harry Mitcheson, the former manager at the yard, who had set up his own business building small boats in the former docks.

Another abiding memory for Joe, now living in retirement in Bohemia Terrace, Blyth, is the cavalcade of bikes which poured out at the twelve o'clock hooter carrying the workmen off for lunch. He was one of them taking advantage of the one hour break.

The bikes were not allowed to be stored inside the yard so hundreds of them were in a cycle park in York Street. There were occasions, however, when he borrowed a bike to run errands for the foreman.

"When platers failed to turn in causing production problems young apprentices were sent to their homes," he said. "I once had to cycle to Tenth Avenue to knock on the door of a plater and say: 'Mr. Rafferty wants to know if you are coming to work'. On this occasion he did turn out."

It was not all sweetness and light at Blyth Shipyard. Pilfering was widespread despite the appointment of Hoot Gibson, a well known retired Blyth policeman, as a security officer. He also kept an eye on workmen trying to leave work before the hooter and allegedly, on one occasion, thrust a baton he carried between the legs of one man trying to get a flyer.

He was not around, however, when metal thievery came into vogue. One worker wrapped so much cable around his body under a coat that he was not able to mount his bicycle. Amid laughter some of his colleagues gave him a hand to get on and cycle off.

Another man, a carpenter, always took his toolbox home on a Friday much to the puzzlement of a friend. Eventually he was asked: "Why do you take your box home on a Friday when you have to carry it back on a Monday." To which he got the reply: "It's not my bl...dy toolbox. It's a block of wood."

Apparently he shaped a large block of top quality wood, used during the fitting out of the interior of the ships, in the carpenters shop every week, painted it the colour of his tool box, and carried it past security.

Pilfering, while on a large scale, did not threaten the future of the yard but the power of the unions, one in particular, the Boilermakers, certainly did. Not only did they negotiate the price when the keel of a ship was laid but they also claimed a launching bonus before the vessel was allowed to slide down the stocks.

I can recall Harry Mitcheson, the manager, telling me off the record when interviewing him for The Journal newspaper after the closure, that he lived almost daily with the constant threat of strike action from all the unions in the yard.

One former worker said: "Demarcation was rife. If a screw needed turning the right union had to provide the man and you waited until he was available. On some occasions there was a queue of men waiting for one man to turn up to do a simple job any of us could have done in seconds."

Another said: "They ran the show and that, I'm sure, helped to close the yard." Whatever the reason the closure helped tear the industrial heart and life out of the town of Blyth.

The last boilermakers – Back row: Sid Wilkinson, Bill McAvoy. Middle row: Ernie Young, Tom McAvoy, Billy Soulsby, Jackie Mann, Mick Shanks, Tommy "Tot" Charlton, George Clifford, Jackie King. Kneeling: David Hall (apprentice).

The Newspapers of Blyth

The Gleaner, the Guardian, the Blyth Echo, the Star, the Examiner, the Scribe, the Daily Post, the Observer – just some of the newspapers launched in Blyth and, hard to believe, there was an Aunty Bessy Help Me column over 150 years ago.

Journalism started in Blyth in 1817 when the Blyth Monthly Gleaner was launched. It was an unusual periodical as it circulated in Newcastle, Morpeth, North Shields and Sunderland as well as in East Northumberland.

It carried a deaths column and in the edition for March, 1818, featured at the top of the deaths list that of the Marquess of Abercorn, Baron Paisley and Viscount Strabane and at the bottom Thomas Reay, late of Seaton Sluice.

The contents included a two part story on Rob Roy, the tide tables for Blyth, a poets corner and readers problems answered by "Bessy of Blyth".

It gave an interesting glimpse of life in the town. In September, 1817, Mr. Guthrie wrote: "Since the establishment of a lock up house here the town is pretty well cleared of those numerous gangs of vagrants which lately infested it."

But Mr. Guthrie was apparently wrong for he published a page of various offences about which he wrote: "It is with unfeigned regret that we notice several disgraceful transactions which have recently been committed here such as breaking windows, interrupting and ill-using females in the street and various other outrages alike disgraceful to human nature."

He went on: "Unless a more efficient police be established and part of the most active of the inhabitants accompany such police in their rounds we fear every other means will prove abortive."

In May of the same year he reported the praiseworthy exertions of "our churchwardens in lately causing two individuals to be put into the lock up house for having been tippling during divine service and for having deterred numbers of boys from gathering together and playing at pitch-halfpenny on Sundays."

The Gleaner also commented on the introduction of the very latest bicycles saying: "Rage for velocipedes still increases and Blyth has got contaminated with the mania. Four of these automats, the workmanship of their several proprietors, may be seen parading about the streets, managed with a dexterity that would do credit to any first rate dandy of the metropolis."

The monthly lasted only two years and there is no record of any other newssheet until February, 1864, when the Blyth Guardian was born. In 1871 it was joined by the Morpeth and Blyth Echo but both went out of existence a year later.

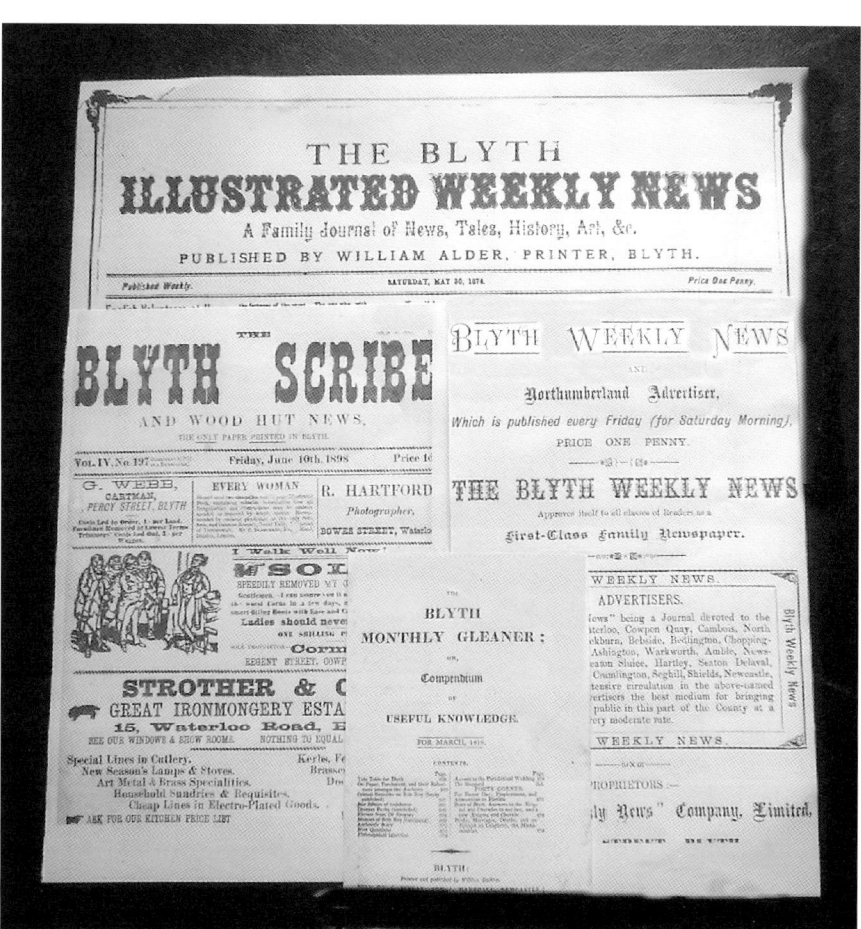

This is a collection of the titles of the papers launched in Blyth.

The year 1874 saw the arrival of three new papers – the Blyth Illustrated Weekly News, the Blyth and Bedlington Star and the Blyth Weekly News.

The Blyth and Bedlington Star had its offices in Waterloo Road and ran for only a year. The Illustrated Weekly News folded the same year and no wonder as under its masthead it described itself as a "Family Journal of News, Tales, History and Art". The news included stories of a shooting competition in France and a murder of a four year old boy in Boston, America. It was published by William Alder, a Blyth printer.

The Blyth Examiner, launched by John Robinson, lasted only six years from 1888 and John Tweedy's Blyth Echo was another paper which had a short life.

The founder of the Blyth Weekly News was a ship owner, Mr. William Alder, whose declared aim was "an essentially local newspaper conducted on broad non-party lines." It ran until 1894 when the Blyth and Wansbeck Telegraph came into being that year. It proved too strong a competitor for the Weekly News which soon went out of business.

The Blyth Daily Scribe also had a sub title " Wood Hut News". One can only assume its office was in such a building. In its 197th. edition on June the 10th., 1898, the Scribe claimed to be the only newspaper printed in the town – the word printed underlined, but obviously not the only one published in the town..

The News, which became the Blyth News and Wansbeck Telegraph in 1894, fought off the challenge of the Scribe and the Blyth Daily Post and Sporting Pilot . It published under that title until 1920 when it became the Blyth News which, in turn, five years later, became the Blyth News and Ashington Post.

The last new paper to be launched in Blyth was the Blyth Weekly Observer and Advertiser. While attempting to compete against the now long established Blyth News and Ashington Post it came out at a most inopportune time – 1939 – and with the outbreak of war quickly disappeared.

The front page of the Blyth News, which published on a Monday and Thursday from an office in Waterloo Road, carried Blyth and Bedlington stories while the front page was changed to carry Ashington and Newbiggin copy produced from an office in Station Road. The former Blyth office is now a retail shop while the Regent Street office, into which the paper moved as a weekly in the 1950's, was swallowed up in the Mall development.

The Blyth News and Ashington Post became the News Post in 1974 then on August 4th, 1982, took its present format, the News Post Leader, delivered free throughout the Blyth area although costing 70 pence if purchased at a newsagents.

The last editor of the Blyth News was Ronnie Cross who served during the Second World War as a tank commander in North Africa. He was a staunch playing member of Blyth Golf Club and following his death in 1994 a trophy, The Ron Cross Pairs Challenge Cup was launched in his name to be played annually

With the advent of computers, mobile phones and electronic news gathering for the first time in 150 years there is no newspaper man or woman based in Blyth. The closure of the Evening Chronicle office in Seaforth Street

Ronnie Cross, the long serving editor of the Blyth News.

and the Blyth News office in Regent Street has brought to an end a period which once saw eleven journalists working in the town. There were enough to form a branch of the National Union of Journalists, and active enough to hold an annual Press Ball in aid of charity in the Roxy Ballroom.

The Tragedy of Blyth's Pianist Prodigy

A Blyth teenager rated the best young pianist in Great Britain after winning scores of competitions and who was awarded a five year free scholarship to a top music college where he was tipped to become an international star, gave it all up on the advice of his doctor. This is the story of Alan Pitkeathley.

Alan, the youngest of five brothers, lived with his parents Bill, a riveter at Blyth Shipyard, and Lillian Pitkeathley in a three bedroomed council house in Fourth Avenue. He attended the nearby Princess Louise Infants School and it was when he moved on to Crofton Junior School that he took up the piano. He was eight at the time and although his father busked on the family piano none of the family could be called musical.

"I have no recollection of asking to play the instrument, it just seemed to happen," said Alan, now a 79-year-old pensioner living in First Avenue.

Elsie Morley, who lived in Cypress Crescent, was his first music teacher. She was delighted to find she had a youngster who thoroughly enjoyed practising and he stayed with her until he was eleven. She told him then that she had taken him as far as she could and recommended Bob Hindmarch, recently demobbed from the RAF, and living in Middleton Street to continue his training.

Bob was such a popular teacher he could only offer Alan a lesson at eight o'clock on a Saturday morning. These early sessions lasted three years when Bob, unfortunately, died at the age of 47.

By now Alan was making a name for himself with wins at competitions in Morpeth, Middlesbrough, Ryton, Darlington and Stockton. His finest victory at that time came with the winning of the Gertrude Ewood Trophy at the North of England festival held in the Old Assembly Rooms in Newcastle. He was thirteen at the time although he was competing in an older age class. Another top award came just a year later with the winning in 1948 of the Journal Trophy before a packed City Hall in Newcastle.

Alan was now being taught by Norman Spowart, who had been a great rival of Bob Hindmarsh, and it meant a two-bus journey for his weekly lessons at Widdrington – not, however, at eight on a Saturday morning.

Alan Pitkeathley.

"I got a bus to Ashington, then took a bus heading to Amble getting off at Widdrington," says Alan. "It took just over an hour each way."

The enthusiasm of his new teacher for his playing led to him being entered in the Blackpool National Music Festival where he was up against almost fifty others in the Under 17 section.

Norman Spowart, who travelled with him, saw him chosen at the Winter Gardens as one of three to go forward to the final at Blackpool Opera House. He was fifteen at the time and his playing won him the Frank Farrand Trophy.

Alan's talent saw him appearing in numerous concerts in and around Blyth including the famous Sunday night shows at the Central and Wallaw cinemas where he played on bills featuring professional artistes.

Even now Alan is embarrassed when he reveals he played in concerts wearing shorts and that included his debut on national radio. It was for a Children's Hour "Young

Artistes" programme and he played three pieces in the Newcastle studio of the BBC. It should have been the first of many appearances on radio and indeed television but as you will learn later it was not to be.

In March, 1957, Alan was awarded a gold medal for getting the highest marks as the top Grade Eight student of any under 17 instrumentalist in Great Britain by the Associate Board of the Royal Schools of Music. He scored 145 out of 150 but he did not receive the medal. Instead he was given a certificate and £50 voucher saying he was a gold medallist in that particular grade.

Before the Second World War the winners were invited to Buckingham Palace to be presented with a gold medal from the King. The practice was stopped in 1939 at the outbreak of hostilities and not resumed.

It was Norman Spowart who entered Alan, then seventeen, for a scholarship at the Royal Manchester College of Music. He travelled down alone by train and found his way to the college where he played Chopin and Debussy for a large examining board and was then asked to sight read a difficult piece.

"I was told I would be informed by letter and it arrived a week or so later to tell me that I had won a free five year scholarship to the college," said Alan. "I was fortunate that a friend of a friend of Norman's had parents who lived in Pendlebury, near Swinton, and they invited me to lodge there. I was astonished to find when I arrived they had a lovely piano although, as they did not play themselves, I think it was brought in especially for me."

Alan began a regime of a couple of days at college each week then at least seven or eight hours practise a day followed by theoretical work. It lasted three years until his worried parents got him to visit Ronnie Dodds, a Blyth doctor and fan of his playing.

Alan became a gold medallist – although all he got was this certificate.

After an extensive examination he concluded Alan, because of the way he was driving himself, was on the brink of a serious nervous breakdown and recommended he withdrew from the college.

Alan took the advice and indeed gave up playing for five years until Brian Lambert, musical director of the newly reformed Blyth Operatic Society, persuaded him in 1959 to become the accompanist.

Three years after resuming Alan met and married May Sweet on October 20th., 1962, musically an unlikely pairing as May was a staunch brass band enthusiast as her father had played in the Cowpen and Crofton Brass Band and she

Alan spent five years away from the piano until he was invited to accompany Blyth Operatic Society. Here he is at the Theatre Royal in Blyth at a rehearsal for The Desert Song in 1963.

could not stand classical music. But the couple went on to have three daughters – Moira and twins Fiona and Elaine. All three took piano lessons from a Mrs. Hornsby on Broadway Circle but all three gave it up.

Alan and May's marriage lasted over 50 years until she died in June, 2013.

Since retiring from playing for the operatic society in 1970, Alan has not touched the keyboard although there is a piano in his home in First Avenue. Asked to pose at the keyboard for a picture for this article he declined although he allowed one taken in his garden.

He said: "I have always regretted having to give up college as I was told at the time I had a future on the classical platform. The college told me my place was always open if I wanted to return which was very nice of them but I was never tempted."

After giving up the piano Alan met and married May.

The Blyth Society moved from the Theatre Royal to the Wallaw Cinema. Here Alan is at rehearsal for Calamity Jane with Albert Lawton conducting and Norman Waddle on sax.

The Two Strong Men of Blyth

Dennis Warnes – Mr. England

At the age of eighteen Dennis, who lived in Jubilee Road, Blyth, saw his first weight-lifting contest and decided then it was the sport for him. Three years later he won six titles at the North of England Amateur Championships.

Dennis Warnes six feet tall, fourteen and a half stone with a 50 inch chest and 30 inch waist went on to win the North British title at the North Counties championship.

While doing his National Service in the Royal Artillery where, appropriately enough, he was a physical training instructor, he continued his body building.

On demobilisation and at the age of twenty three Dennis was crowned Mr. England and became so popular that Blyth Grammar schoolgirls would congregate on the Links on a Sunday afternoon just to see Dennis in his shorts on his training run.

One of the girls, now in her 70's, who did not want to be named, said; "He was a real pin up for us. We would have a coffee in the Jubilee Café and wait for him to come by in the briefest of shorts and no top."

Dennis was first employed by Blyth Co-operative Society in their works department as a journeyman – a job which was interrupted by the call to do his National Service.

Bill Cox was an apprentice painter and decorator with the Co-op Building Department in Croft Road in 1958 and remembers the time when former employees returned from doing their National Service.

He said: "One Monday morning we turned up for our work sheets and found a new face in the department who was built like a man mountain – it was Dennis. We found him to be quite easy going and a pleasure to work with compared to some of the others who'd returned, particularly those from the navy.

Dennis Warnes in a competition pose.

"Dennis was what was known as a journeyman who was skilled at graining, particularly the figure cut style. During our free time he used to challenge the apprentices to try and pin him down. We never succeeded, he was always too quick and of course he had tremendous upper body strength."

Dennis, for a time, tried his hand at wrestling and fought at St. James Hall, Newcastle, under his own name along with another Blyth lad, the late Tommy Morrison who fought as Tony Lord. The pair travelled to venues throughout the North East.

Dennis then became a fire fighter at the Morpeth station but also tried his hand as an insurance man and then a swimming instructor at Blyth Sports Centre. It was from there he was attached to the training pool which had been installed at the Blyth Grammar School in Plessey Road. It had been decided that all children in Northumberland should be taught to swim and he taught hundreds before the baths were closed during the Margaret Thatcher years.

Bill Cox.

By now Dennis was married to Pat who although a teacher was also into body building and she won the Miss England title. They lived in a bungalow overlooking the harbour at Seaton Sluice but later bought a house in Whitley Bay.

From there they eventually moved to America and settled in Florida where, it has been reported, they set up a school. It would appear to have been such a success they could afford to buy a holiday home in Barbados.

Dennis, 74, and Pat now live in Maidstone, Kent, but enjoy lengthy, extended holidays, particularly during the winter, in Barbados.

Dennis and Pat, his wife, who also won the Miss England competition.

Strong Man No. 2 – Willie Carr

Willie Carr, the "Samson of England" and reputed to be the strongest man in the world was born on April 3rd, 1756, at a hamlet near Old Hartley but moved with his family soon afterwards to Blyth.

As his father was a master blacksmith it was natural for him to follow him into the trade. And no wonder for at the age of 17 he stood almost six feet, four inches tall, and weighed 18 stone. He could lift seven or eight hundredweights and throw a 60 lb. weight 24 feet.

Willie Carr was 24 stones by the age of 30, a quiet, handsome man, perfectly developed, deep chested with muscular broad shoulders. He was known to have lost his temper only twice in his life. Once when struck with a whip for no reason by Lord Haddo, a Scottish nobleman, at Morpeth races. Willie picked the man out of the saddle and shook him until the he screamed an apology.

The second occasion was when two drunken sailors started to quarrel and fight outside his house as his wife lay dying. When the men refused to go away or stop he picked them up by their necks, one in each hand, and banged their heads together until they yelled for mercy much to the amusement of a crowd which had gathered.

Willie was very popular with gentry and nobility and was a regular visitor to Seaton Delaval Hall where he entertained Lord Delaval and guests with feats of strength.

On one occasion Big Ben, a famous bare-fisted fighter, was a visitor to the Hall and Lord Delaval arranged for Willie to fight him. When the pair shook hands Willie squeezed so hard the blood oozed from Ben's finger tips. He then refused to go on with the match saying he would rather be kicked by a horse than take a blow from such a hand.

Blyth's Goliath would often demonstrate his strength in his local hostelry.

Willie's strength was such that five sailors were unable to carry an anchor for repair. Willie was sent for, picked it up, and to their amazement carried it easily to his father's smithy.

Etching of Willie carrying the anchor.

On another occasion Willie was overwhelmed and captured by a large Naval press gang stationed at Blyth during the American War of Independence. With his hands tied he was hustled into a rowing boat. But it had hardly left the jetty when, bracing his shoulders against one side and his feet against the other he smashed the boat and in the confusion escaped. He also showed his prodigious strength by picking up an eight-stone girl and leaping a five barred gate with her in his arms.

On the death of his father Willie took over the business and gained a reputation for making fine, exceptionally strong harpoons. This led to an event which sealed his reputation as the strongest man when he carried a box of the weapons weighing one hundredweight from Blyth to North Shields to fulfil an order after missing the early morning carrier. It is reported that he drank 84 glasses of gin on the way but returned home that night perfectly sober.

Lord Delaval was so taken by Willie that he had his portrait painted wearing his blacksmith's working clothes and a horned Viking helmet. The painting hung for years in the hall but was apparently moved to another hall and despite extensive searches by the National Trust volunteers no trace of it can be found.

Willie Carr suffered a stroke in 1818 and for the next ten years, until his death at the age of 68, rarely left his bed. A widower, he had no sons and the Carr name died with him. He did, however, have two daughters who lived in the town under their married names of Fenwick and Simpson.

He might not have been Mr. England but there is no doubt if the contest had been held then he would have walked the Mr. Universe title.

An etching shows Willie leaping the gate with the young maiden in his arms.

Blyth's Singing Teenager

From Gilbert and Sullivan to the Toby Twirl pop group; sword fighting on Bamburgh beach; BBC bias against Northern groups and rubbing shoulders with the top stars – all part of the life of a pop star from Blyth in the Swinging Sixties.

It was Gilbert and Sullivan who launched the singing career of Dave "Holly" Holland when he was a pupil at Newlands School in Blyth, now the site of the Bede Academy. But even then he showed his independence when clashing with Tom Easton, one of his teachers, a firm G. & S. traditionalist who produced Pirates of Penzance and Iolanthe which featured the budding pop star.

As Dave says: "As the Pirate King I thought the music should be brought up to the sixties and sang my own version of his main song. Tom did not agree and we had quite a lively discussion. I sang it my way."

Out of school hours Dave and friends got stage experience by appearing in church halls miming to the latest Beatles hits. It paid off for him for while he was a 16-year-old engineering student at Ashington Technical College he was asked to be lead singer in a group to be called Holly and The Acorns.

It was a group which now performed live in those church halls and on gigs including Blyth's non alcoholic night club, the Barbarossa, frequented by youngsters. His talent was soon spotted and led to an invitation to join the more established group, "Shades of Blue", as lead singer. He actually took over from another Blyth lad, the late Graham Bell, who went on to sing with bands in the south of England and abroad.

The group then made such a name for themselves that a talent scout recommended them to the Decca record company. They travelled to London where, after an audition, they were awarded a contract.

Dave "Holly" Holland who celebrated his 65th birthday in August, 2013.

They had, however, to say goodbye to the name "Shades of Blue" as it clashed with an American group and hello to "Toby Twirl". None of the band – Barry Sewell (keyboards), Nick Thorburn (guitar), Stuart Somerville (bass), John Reed (drums) and Dave (vocals), argued about the new name as they were about to launch their first record.

Toby Twirl in a sombre mood on this publicity still.

It was a double A side – "Back in Time" and "Harry Faversham" – and led to them being taken to Bamburgh Castle for a film shoot which involved them riding horses and sword fighting each other for the hand of a beautiful lady, a model hired for the occasion. They were also filmed on Cullercoats beach surrounded by children from a local school and being driven through Newcastle in an open landau. This generated tremendous coverage in local and national papers and the front page of the New Musical Express.

The subsequent film promoting the disc was shown on the popular Tony Blackburn Show where Dave found himself part of a discussion group with Blackburn, Eric Burdon, Sandy Shaw and P.J. Proby.

Despite the tremendous publicity the record failed to register in the charts which Dave puts down to the bias of the radio moguls of the BBC. "The record buying public at that time was led by radio," he said, "if you did not get airplay on that medium you did not make the charts.

"It was not just us. There were a lot of good groups in the North East at the time who were not given a break by the BBC, the exception being The Animals."

Toby Twirl's other records, "Toffee Apple Sunday" and "Movin' In" were released but with the same result although by now the group had been spotted by executives of the Bailey Organisation which operated night clubs throughout the country.

They were persuaded to develop a cabaret act, which included close harmony numbers and comedy, and so began three years of touring the major Bailey clubs around Britain and many other venues. These included the Dolce Vita in Newcastle and Wetheralls in Sunderland.

"There were some very good clubs and there were some stinkers," said Dave.

"At the better ones we found ourselves supporting big name acts like Tommy Cooper, Tom Jones, Dusty Springfield and Bob Monkhouse."

They also made it to London when they found themselves booked into the famous Playboy Club which boasted the most beautiful "bunny" girls complete with tails. "That was quite a visual experience," said Dave.

Extended engagements at clubs with their cabaret act did not stop

The group was dressed up in 18th century finery for the film shoot to go with launch of their record Harry Fashersham. They wore the 18th century garb to ride horses and enact fight scenes on the beach near Bamburgh Castle.

Toby Twirl playing their blues and rock and roll set at gigs on their Sunday nights off. Some club owners though were determined to get their moneys worth. Including the man who booked them for a short season at the Kingsway Casino in Southport. The club was closed on the Sunday but the owner transferred the boys to a nearby cinema he used as a bingo hall.

"We were half way through our act," recalls drummer John Reid, "when the audience, mostly pensioners, got out of their seats and started to run towards the stage. I thought we were going to get invaded. Was this Saga Mania I asked myself?

"Being at the back of the stage on the drums I hadn't seen the Bingo Hall staff emerge into what was the orchestra pit at the front of the stage and start serving free pies and peas which were included in the price of admission. The term 'Pies have come' certainly had a new meaning from that moment on."

Ironically, in view of the lack of airtime on the BBC when their records were released, Toby Twirl were later invited to the BBC Playhouse where they recorded several tracks in a number of three hour sessions. They were later played on the fledgling Radio One. Even now some forty years later they can still be heard on nostalgia programmes and on compilation records. Brian Matthews played two of the group's records on his programme to celebrate Dave's 60th birthday and quite recently "Toffee Apple Sunday" was aired 22 times in six months. Only recently Dave learned they had been included on one compilation disc along with the Bee Gees.

Royalties, however, don't come into it although two of the group Nick and John who wrote some of the songs still occasionally receive cheques.

Tragedy was to strike the group when Stuart, the bass player, was drowned off Tynemouth. His body was never found. Shortly afterwards Toby Twirl disbanded.

Dave married in 1973 and in 1998 gave up his factory job and entered the pub trade by taking over the Joiners Arms in Blyth. He managed it for almost thirteen years until his retirement in 2011.

Although he left the group two years before it disbanded Dave is still on good terms with Barry, Mick and John and they have been together on a number of occasions, the last being his 65th birthday party at the Blyth Constitutional Club in August, 2013.

One top booking for Toby Twirl was at the famous Playboy Club in London. Here they are pictured entering the stage door before meeting the bunny girls.

And it was at that party Dave showed he had lost none of his vocalising when he took to the Karaoke to sing a particular favourite and most requested of his fans – "Everlasting Love."

Nick Thorburn, the lead guitarist, now retired and living in Tynemouth asked about the group said: "We were a good band and probably deserved better. When I listen to some of the 45's that made the charts at the time we were recording I found it hard to believe we did not make it."

Dave added: "Although we felt we did not get the financial rewards we expected it was a very enjoyable time. We were all young and being paid for something we really loved doing. I have lots of memories of fantastic days when fun was fun and music was at its best."

And the internet proves they still have loyal fans, and indeed some new ones, by the number posting messages and queries on the Toby Twirl website.

Toby Twirl were famous throughout the top clubs in the country. Here they are outside the Poco Poco nightclub in Manchester.

38

The Blyth Oriana Choir

The choir conductor who travelled hundreds of miles by car, bus and bicycle to rehearsals in Blyth; the beer drinkers who objected to listening to Mozart and Handel and the man who turned up to singing practice only hours after the death of his wife. All part of the fascinating history of Blyth's most popular choir, the Oriana.

The Blyth Oriana Choir came into being in 1925 thanks to the efforts of the curate of St. Mary's Church in the town the Rev. Herbert Popple, a gifted musician and composer. He set about seeking enough singers to form a group to perform religious and secular music and it was not long before he succeeded. He found enough enthusiasts to start rehearsals in St. Mary's Hall where the first concerts were held on a prefabricated wooden stage made by Robert Shanks, one of the singers.

The Rev. Popple, however, left after four years to become a curate at a church in London but as a farewell gift he gave the choir one of his compositions – "The Triumphs of Oriana". It was an anthem which was aired a number of times by the choir over the early years and a copy can now be seen in Blyth Library.

The departure of the Rev. Popple was followed by the appointment of Mr. William R. James of Low Fell. Although a science teacher at Gateshead Grammar School, later to become headmaster of Heathfield School, also in Gateshead. He was a brilliant musician which he constantly proved during the 52 years he led the choir from 1929 until it's demise in 1981.

At the start of the Second World War the choir voted to carry on with its regular Sunday rehearsals although no concerts would be given during the duration.

Transport problems arose for Mr. James when his school, within close bombing distance of the Tyne, was evacuated to Chester-le-Street. With the extra distance and a vastly reduced wartime bus service, he opted to cycle to Blyth to guarantee he was able to attend at least one rehearsal in three. After a brief rest he cycled back to his school across the Tyne immediately after the rehearsal.

The Blyth Oriana Choir's Silver Jubilee Concert.

When Mr. James was absent the baton was taken by Miss Gladys Smith, a Blyth singing teacher, who was also a member of the Oriana.

The ending of the war meant he was able to continue his bus journeys which involved a change at the Haymarket in Newcastle and attend every rehearsal. He only missed two – both caused when the buses could not run because of fog.

Photocopying of published music is illegal but Mr. James spent many a night copying out by hand in black ink the four parts of a piece – soprano, alto, tenor and bass lines – for every member of the choir. He knew such copying by hand was legal. Another incident showed the dedication Mr. James had to the choir. His wife died on a Sunday morning but he travelled to the rehearsal hours later telling officials there was nothing more he could do at his home.

During the 50 years of the choir's existence there were only ever three accompanists – Mrs. Doris Hornsby, Mrs. Sheila Welsh and Mr. Arnold Clegg, a highly regarded pianist and organist..

The appointment of Mr. Clegg was ideal for Mr. James as they both lived in Low Fell and he was able to dispense with the two buses to Blyth by getting a lift in the accompanist's car.

The popularity of the choir was shown in the number of concerts they held at various venues – two of the most popular being the Presbyterian Church in Waterloo Road, which staged Handels "Messiah", and the Central Methodist Church which stood in those days next to the Bus Station.

Although never boasting a membership of more than forty-five the quality of the music was such they were invited to give concerts throughout Northumberland and Durham often with professional guest singers such at Owen Brannigan and Kenneth Ormston. Brinkburn Priory in the early fifties was one venue which followed concerts at Monkwearmouth Monastery and Hexham Abbey.

The choir performing in Elizabethan costumes at Bywell church in 1960.

In 1961 members of the choir dressed in Elizabethan costumes to perform madrigals at Bywell in the Tyne Valley and later that decade developed an association with a church at Blackhall in County Durham which led to a series of concerts there.

Two of the Oriana went on to achieve national reputations as soloists. They were James Charlton and Anne Guthrie. But one whose remarkable voice could only be heard in the concerts because of family commitments was Kathleen Moorhead. Mr. James said had she been given the opportunity, she could have achieved the same recognition as Kathleen Ferrier.

In the late 1960's the choir began to rehearse in the upper room of the Mason's Arms in Plessey Road on a peppercorn rent and where the manager also provided them with a cupboard in which they could store the music.

He also fended off regular complaints from the drinkers in the bar directly under the rehearsal room. They did not appreciate Mozart, Byrd and Handel with their pints!

In 1975 a dinner was held in the Star and Garter Hotel to mark the 50th th anniversary of the choir and two years later another dinner was held this time to mark the 50 years Mr. James had been the conductor. So unique was this achievement it merited a mention in a national newspaper.

Three years after that celebration came a threat to the existence of the choir when a new manager of the Masons Arms brought their tenure to a close saying their room was going to be redeveloped. Although the choir was invited to use the newly developed Phoenix Theatre free of charge a special meeting was held by the existing twelve choir members, all of whom were getting on in years, when it was decided to disband.

George Robson, the last secretary, a position he held for thirteen years, was instructed to give the choir's comprehensive music collection to the Northumberland County Library at Morpeth where it stayed until it was destroyed in the devastating Morpeth floods of 2008.

Bill Sullivan, a long standing member of the choir, at the final meeting, invited the remaining members to attend a Christmas reunion at his home in Roseberry Avenue. and three such reunions were held in succeeding years when carols and other seasonal music were lustily sung.

They too came to an end with the death of Mr. James, at the age of 82, in 1984 at a rest home in Whitley Bay where he had moved from Low Fell after retirement from his headship.

The choir in the Star and Garter in 1977 celebrating Mr. James 60th season as a conductor. Back Row: Mr. Sproson, Ted Dunne, Jack Fairbairn, Bill Sullivan, Mr. Wilson. Middle Row: Una Locke, Mrs. Sproson, Mrs. Dunne, Mr. Jewels, May Jewels, Mercia Wilson, Mrs. Henderson, Miss Thomas, Olive Morris, Daz Raffle, Kathleen Moorhead, ????, Danny White. Front row: George Robson (secretary), Arnold Clegg, Rev. Marks, Mr. W. James (conductor), Mrs. May Durrant, Vivienne Jackson, Miss James.

The Youth Club Author

Preacher, musician, cricketer, actor, author and youth leader -titles which can all be ascribed to Charles "Charlie" Mills – one of the outstanding personalities to come out of the town of Blyth in the last century.

Charlie first saw the light of day on November 22nd., 1919, in Wood Street – the third child of James and Georgina Mills. His father, a miner, was a noted gymnast, bandsman in the Boys Brigade and a staunch member of the Zion Methodist Church in Waterloo Road, now part of Blyth Market Place.

James Mills was a huge influence on his son and Charlie followed him into the Boys Brigade, where he eventually became an officer. He also joined the band where he was taught the euphonium and sang in the brigade choir.

At the age of 14 Charlie went to work as an apprentice colliery blacksmith, a trade he followed for three years before, in 1937, he switched to Blyth shipyard as an apprentice carpenter and liner-off from which he transferred to the draughtsman's office where he stayed for 12 years, missing service in the Second World War as he was in a reserved occupation.

Charlie Mills at his desk.

It was during the war he became a founder member of the Blyth Phoenix Dramatic Society playing the lead in many plays including Rebecca and Claudia. It was in November, 1942, he married his childhood sweetheart, Dorothy Lawrence, after a six year courtship. Charlie could pick them, for his bride was a former Blyth Carnival Rose winner.

It was a union to be blessed with two sons, Graham and David and two daughters, Marie and Denise.

Apart from his interest in drama Charlie was a keen cricketer and in 1944 helped organise the Blyth Tradesmens Cricket League which included teams from Bates Pit, the Welwyn factory, the Co-op, Blyth Phoenix, Blyth Shipyard and many others and played matches on pitches on Broadway, Cowpen and Isabella.

It was a tremendous success and ran well into the Fifties blooding youngsters who went on to play for Blyth Cricket Club in the Northumberland League.

Dorothy Mills.

The year 1949 saw Charlie change careers for the last time when he spotted an advertisement in the Blyth News seeking a leader for the Town Boys Club. Although told someone had already been chosen for the job he still applied and found at his interview that the chairman of the panel was none other than the shipyard manager Bill Turnbull.

He asked searching questions such as why he wanted to take a job which offered half the salary he was getting at the yard. His response he felt it was a calling got him the job and so began the start of a lifetime in youth work.

Charlie held the position at the Boys Club for three years until asked if he would take over the Blyth YMCA. The Christian aspect of the work held a great appeal for him so he, his wife and family, moved into the flat above the YMCA in Waterloo Road where they stayed for four years. His post at the Boys Club was taken by Jack Allen which he held for 24 years.

Charlie's new job proved to be a 24 hours a day one, particularly with living above the YMCA with members having easy access to him. But he managed to have a break during the afternoon by following his love of the movies.

Bart Kinnair, the then chairman, always said he could not get a hold of him after lunch, as he was at matinees at one of the four cinemas in the town.

Charlie's success in the job was such that in 1956 he was asked if he would launch a new YMCA branch in Bishop Auckland. It was a challenge he accepted and his recruiting drive was such – visiting schools, factories and organisations – that the branch eventually boasted over 300 members and had a board of governors which included top business and banking people from the area.

His success was all the more remarkable as some of the members were the hardest, toughest type of youngsters imaginable.

The Princess Royal, Princess Anne, attended the opening ceremony and in the same year he met the Duke of Edinburgh at the Framwellgate Moor Grammar School as part of his work with the Duke's Award Scheme.

Six years at Bishop Auckland was followed by a posting to Bargoed YMCA in South Wales which was a mixed branch with the girls having their own leader. After four years, however, Dorothy was homesick for the North East and thanks to the efforts of Miss Valerie Tully, the Northumberland County Youth Organiser, Charlie took over the Ashington YMCA in 1984 where his running of the club soccer team saw it win the Welfare League the following season. He started a drama group and it was then he began writing his own Geordie plays, all with a local theme. They proved

Charlie and the Duke of Edinburgh

tremendously successful with him calling on occasions on some of his acting friends from Blyth to take part in the usually crowded YMCA hall.

Alf and Doreen Douglas travelled from Blyth to take part in some of the plays and Alf recalls one amusing incident involving Doreen.

"Her part involved her in wearing a several strings of beads and it was while she was coming down the stairs in one scene they snapped causing mayhem as they scattered all over the stage risking the life and limb of the rest of the cast."

Charlie then branched out into pantomimes which proved a great source of income for his YMCA. In all he wrote six plays and eight Christmas shows.

Although born in Blyth Charlie did not make many visits to his home town even when he settled in Ashington. But as a member of the Ashington YMCA snooker team he returned to his former club Blyth to play, and win, all their matches.

Gerry Evans was in charge of the Blyth club and tells of how good Charlie was as a snooker player. "We did not stand a chance for also in his three man team was the Northumberland snooker champion."

But Gerry recalls the time Charlie brought his soccer team to play the Blyth YMCA. "He might have trounced us at snooker but we hammered his side 4-2 at soccer."

One of Charlie's return visits is still remembered by those who attended a certain Burns Night held at the Star and Garter Hotel.

Charlie was invited to reply to the toast to the Haggis and he did with a poem he had written titled "Whatever Happened to Good Old Blyth." You will find it below with some slight updating.

Apart from his work in the YMCA Charlie was a well-known preacher in local churches, spoke at many organisations and was actively involved in many voluntary bodies including those dealing with the deaf and blind. He also formed an entertainments group called "Charlie's Angels" which toured hundreds of venues including old peoples homes, sheltered accommodation and luncheon clubs.

Just some of the pantos Charlie wrote.

Charlie spent 20 years at Ashington until his retirement in November, 1984.

He died on 25th, July, 1995, but his wife Dorothy, at 90 is still extremely active and attends an afternoon club at Lynemouth Day Centre three times a week. She lives in the family home in Ellington and is in regular touch with her seven grandchildren, nine great grandchildren and two great, great, grandchildren.

Whatever Happened to Good Old Blyth?
By Charlie Mills

Whatever happened to good old Blyth when Hoot Gibson walked the beat?
And the lads played Muddy Kuddy and Relieve in the street.
When Blyth had a passenger service on a popular railway line,
And the bus fare to Newcastle was a paltry one and nine.

When neighbours used to really care and ask if you were coping.
And you went and did your shopping and left the back door open.
Hedley and Young's was a classy shop and Skees sold goods for sailors.
And men could get a really good suit from the Forty Shilling tailors.

There was Willsy Herron the optician selling specs at a moderate price.
And almost right opposite, the chemist's called Fordyce.
Sad to recall the churches, which all seemed to be fading and dying,
Regent Street, Bowes Street and Beaconsfield, and the last to go was Zion.

Whatever happened to good old Blyth before we got flashy new clubs.
And Sunday was a day for church instead of crowding into pubs.
Most of our cinemas had to close down when interest in Bingo grew,
The Essoldo, Roxy and Theatre Royal and the Central Cinema too.
Remember the Tudor Ballroom where you could get a really good dance,
And the young men and women behaved themselves, and found time for love and romance.

The miners worked hard for their money, and got six and ninepence a shift.
With big families to feed the miners wives all knew the meaning of thrift.
The men coming home in their work gear, black faced through the colliery gate,
With the little bairns shouting "have you got any left over bait?"

Stotties

The women always baked their own bread, with a master baker's skill,
Ahhh the smell of freshly baked stotties as they cooled on the window sill.
Everybody worked hard in the family but still found time for chit chat,
And neighbour would come and help you finish off your proggy mat.
There were smiles galore at the allotments as they planted turnips and tetties,
But by gum it was cold on a winter's night when you crossed the yard to the netties.

The Alexandra Billiard Hall with the Mounts looking after the games,
Of billiards and snooker and Russian Pool and others with more fancy names.
Will you ever forget Ballast Hill with Boyd's Dairy and Boast's chandler's shop,
And the dreary prison-like Lodging House where the homeless and tramps would flop.

The shipyard was fully employed then, working on ships old and new,
And hundreds of bikes flew down Regent Street when the shipyard buzzer blew.
The bakers used to have biscuit boys roaming around the streets,
And their cries could be heard quite clearly selling their buns or "bisceets".
Teachers taught and ruled at school with a cane that stung the hand,
And those who set their cheek up were well and truly tanned.

Sunday Tea

The Sunday tea was quite a treat, bread and butter and lemon curd,
And the children were strictly disciplined and "seen" but seldom "heard".
They were out and entertained themselves, no fear of vandals or cosh,
Then into the tub for their weekly bath when their Mothers had finished the wash.
We now have Asda and Morrisons and other cut price stores,
Which have squeezed out all the little shops which flourished between the wars.

But things have to change, or so we are told, progress will not be denied.
Although quite a few of the new-fangled things, the old ones cannot abide.
Of course there are ideals and qualities which will forever with us stay,
Like love and friendship and little kindnesses which can brighten up our day.
So the next time we sigh for the "good old days" when everything seemed to be fine,
Remember we don't have to change our standards – that choice is yours and mine.

Whatever happened to good old Blyth?
Well places and folk change, of course.
But if we ARE to change, we must make sure,
The change is better, not for worse.

Wellesley Nautical School

The Wellesley boy who became hairdresser to Royalty; the young burglars who found a dead body and the bully who saved the life of one of his victims, all stories during the eighty years the Wellesley Nautical School was a feature of life in Blyth.

The Wellesley Nautical School was started in 1868 not in Blyth but thirteen miles south on the Tyne. A group of philanthropic businessmen, led by a James Hall, launched a scheme to provide accommodation and training for young men, including waifs, with a view to them serving in the Royal and Merchant navies.

The first Wellesley was on board HMS Cornwall, a ship of the line which was built in India and boasted 74 guns. It only lasted six years when it was replaced by HMS Boscawen which was moored at North Shields and was renamed Training Ship Wellesley.

Early last century it had broadened the catchment area of Tyneside and North Yorkshire for trainees by accepting boys from London, Manchester and Liverpool.

The TS Wellesley was destroyed by fire on March 11th, 1914, although the 300 boys were evacuated without any injuries. They were to spend the next four years in the Tynemouth Plaza building.

Training Ship Wellesley.

The Wellesley on fire at North Shields

A large site at Blyth, which had been used as a submarine base to house crews and support workers at the port during the First World War, was earmarked for the school.

TS Wellesley was run by the Wellesley Trust which was composed of a number of public spirited people. The Trust launched a public appeal which raised £22,000 towards the purchase of the site helped by the Government who contributed existing buildings there and the generosity of Blyth Council in donating a parcel of attached land to seal the deal.

Route marches in full uniform were a regular part of the training programme at the school. Here the boys can be seen on a march along the coast towards Blyth.

Wellesley was used as a navy training school until 1933 but then became an approved school although it continued to train boys, some of whom were abandoned children, in trades which allowed them to join ships sailing out of Blyth.

Forty years later Wellesley became a Community Home with Education when it was taken over by the Social Services department of Sunderland Council and there was a gradual move away from training for the sea in the 1980's.

Prince George, Duke of Kent visited Wellesley in October, 1933 Ald. Aaron Walton, the Mayor Blyth is to the right. The prince died in an air crash in Scotland in 1942.

It was in 1973 that Les Fay joined the staff as a house master rising eventually to duty officer under the leadership of Captain Don Swanston.

Les, who is 71, and retired, living at Seaton Sluice, was also a member of the Blyth RNLI and found himself on one occasion on board the inshore lifeboat, having to help rescue six of his boys and a staff member from Blyth Bay.

The school had a sailing lugger which was used for seamanship training and one Saturday afternoon an instructor, new to the base, took six of the boys fishing.

On returning to port the boat was overturned by a large wave. All seven on board were wearing life jackets and managed to hang on to the hull. Unfortunately one of the boys, a Pakistani teenager from Middlesbrough, was washed off the boat and swept away. Another boy immediately swam after him and held him until the pilot cutter, which had also responded to the alarm, collected them from the sea. In the meantime Les and his fellow RNLI crew rescued the other five.

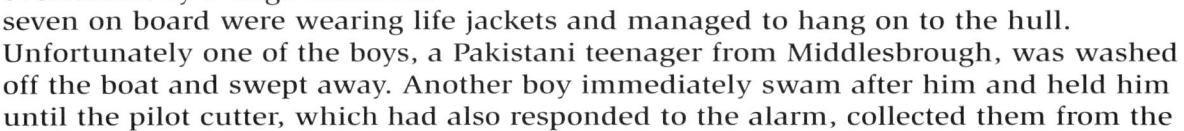

Captain Swanston in 1969

Describing the rescue Les said: "I never ceased to be amazed at the boys during my time at the school. On this occasion for instance, the Pakistani lad who had been swept away was small and scrawny and had been bullied mercilessly. But the worst bully was the one who went after and saved him.

"A week later that same lad, the hero, stole a car and was decapitated when he crashed into the rear of a heavy goods lorry."

One of the features of town life in Blyth for many years was the sound of the Wellesley Bugle Band on Sunday mornings after the Second World War when the school marched to services at St. Cuthbert's Church.

Les Fay.

And church was not the only place they were marched to. Those that behaved themselves were taken to the cinema. Later, however, when Wellesley was run by Sunderland Council the boys could come and go as they pleased and this led to a ban in 2003 of all the pupils from the Wallaw, the last cinema in town. Two of the boys had got into one of the three projection rooms, which was unmanned at the time, and cut the film as it was running through the projector.

Throughout the early years the school tried to integrate itself in the life of the town and had a regular float in the Blyth Carnival but it was a losing battle as there were regular protests from people about break ins and vandalism.

On one occasion three of the boys broke into a house

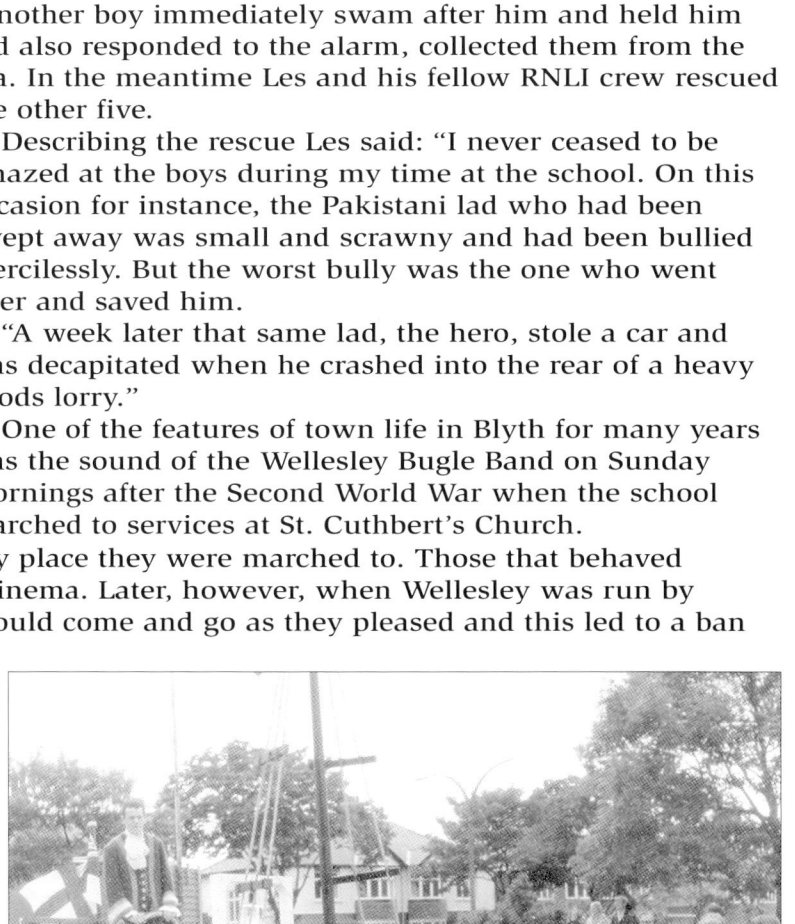

The school entered a float each year in the Blyth Carnival – this was one of the entries which reflected the work of the Wellesley.

near the school not knowing the owner was lying dead from natural causes in an upstairs bedroom. After stealing bottles of spirits from a drinks cabinet they went upstairs and discovered the body.

They covered his face with a sheet and took the drinks back to the school where they held a party in the dormitory. When staff learned of the incident, the police were called and the three boys arrested. They were charged with burglary and eventually sent for trial at the Crown Court in Newcastle.

Les Fay went to court and after he explained a return to Wellesley would be the most advantageous for their future of the boys the judge agreed.

Blyth-born Ian Woodhouse, who was a housemaster for 11 years at the school said: "There was a lot going on. Apart from lessons there was a tremendous amount of sport – football, cricket and especially boxing.

"There were so many good boxers that matches were held in the school gymnasium against Wallsend Boys Club, which was also noted at the time for its fighters."

Ian, now 70 and living in retirement in Twenty Third Avenue, added: "One of the worst punishments for a boy was to be banned from boxing. We had some wild ones but the majority behaved themselves and I know a lot of them became model citizens."

One of the boys went on to be hairdresser to Princes Margaret and returned to the school to proudly show the pass which gave him access to Buckingham Palace.

Les Jay said: "There were other successes in putting the boys on the right path but there were also failures some who committed murder after leaving."

In May. 1988, the Commander, Jake Patrick, wrote in the school magazine: "Even in my short life at Wellesley I am aware of a great many boys who have attained a great deal and are a credit to the school and the staff. These 'old boys' continue to remain firm friends of the school and look back on their days at Wellesley with no regrets."

Admiral Collingwood 50 foot Training Yacht

An example of old boy success was George Nicholson (1938-40), who arrived at the school in June, 1988, in a white Rolls Royce for the unveiling of a memorial he had sponsored to those from the school who died in the Second World War.

At the other end of the spectrum was a story which unfolded during a case history conference at the school involving a North East boy. His father and brother attended the meeting at which they were told that the boy was to get an apprenticeship in the engineering section. At this the brother said: "But he's already got an apprenticeship." This came as a surprise to the staff as nothing was showing in the records. When asked what the apprenticeship was the brother replied in all earnest: "Whey he's an apprentice burglar." The family, which consisted of eight sons, were notorious in their area for their criminal activities and all had convictions.

The end of the school came after Blyth Borough Council refused Sunderland planning permission to make improvements to the site and although the Wearside authority eventually won an appeal they decided not to go ahead with the plan and Wellesley closed in November, 2006.

When it was announced the school was closing a couple of the wilder boys decided to celebrate by removing tiles off the roof of the little cottage at the entrance and using them as missiles aiming particularly at the figurehead which stood near the entrance. The site stood empty for almost seven years but eventually was sold to a building firm for luxury housing.

The Wellesley Figurehead

The five foot tall wooden carved figurehead of Admiral Boscawen, who gave his name to HMS Boscawen, was a prominent feature just inside the entrance to the school. The Boscawen was the ship tied up at North Shields which served as the school for 40 years.

When the ship, which had been renamed the Wellesley, was destroyed by fire in 1914 the figurehead was moved with the school to Blyth in 1922. It stayed there until it was affected by rot when it was replaced in 1991. The second figurehead was carved by two Newcastle University students, Martyn Grubb and Jayne Bransby who later married. This was on show until the closure of the school in 2006 when, after suffering from vandalism, it was placed in storage.

The Wellesley Figurehead. After its travels from the school to Ashington and then back to a Blyth private house the Wellesley figurehead is now fronting a riverside café.

Three years later, after a request from a former Wellesley boy, the Wellesley Trustees decided to place it on a more fitting site – the Training Ship Tenacity which was the sea cadets headquarters at Ashington. But before this could be done a group of ex-Wellesley trainees supervised by Richard Hunter, a renowned restorer, repaired the vandalism and neglect on the figurehead.

Handover

On January 23rd, 2010, the official handover by Captain R.D. Swanston, retired commanding officer of the Wellesley Nautical School took place. Unfortunately the replacement was neglected and after being found to be covered in green moss was moved by former Wellesley Boys to the garden of a private house, some 50 yards from the school site.

In 2013 it was moved again. It now stands outside a riverside café set up by the volunteers who man the Blyth Volunteer Lifeboat, an organisation set up when, in 2005, the RNLI replaced its sea-going lifeboat with a smaller inshore craft in a cost-cutting exercise.

Capt Swanston after his retirement

The Music Makers of Blyth

Twenty five pence for a night's playing; the double bass fiasco on the top of an Austin Seven; the last minute replacement who won top prizes at a contest and the paid musician who could only play two tunes. All stories from the period when Blyth was a centre for musicians and dance bands.

It is quite hard to believe nowadays that Blyth boasted several bands, numerous places in which dances could be held and enough musicians, sixty of them, to form a branch of the Musicians Union.

But that certainly was the case in the 1930's and 40's and it was all due to the proliferation of players out of the colliery and railway bands. There was only one draw back, there were not sufficient reed players – saxophonists and clarinettists.

John Stenhouse, now 90, who ran a big band and smaller groups for over 60 years in the area said: "The problem was overcome in the main by musicians on other instruments teaching themselves the sax. A case in point being Norman Waddle, a violinist, who joined my band in 1940 when we were playing at St. Wilfrid's church Hall. He soon switched to alto-sax after teaching himself and this became his main instrument.

"Johnny Adams joined the band about the same time initially on trumpet but he switched to tenor sax and so I was able to field a full sax section. Bobby Thompson (Lacker) Thompson on first alto, Norman on second and Johnnie Adams on tenor.

"We also had Arnold Tweedy on first trumpet, having moved from cornet with the LNER Brass Band, Ronny Bailey on second trumpet and Duggie Bradford on trombone with Peter Mortakis on drums completing the line up. Some of these musicians later joined Tommy Bell at the Roxy when he returned from war service."

Norman Waddle.

Johnny recalls when playing with the Kevin McLoughlin band at the St. Cuthberts Dance Club in St. Cuthbert's Church Hall becoming bored playing the old time dances to the same tunes every week.

He said: "The Lancers lasted about twenty minutes with the same tune being played. I went out and re-wrote the music using more modern numbers and we played this the next week. There was uproar and we had to revert to the original music. It was then I realised the dancers weren't as much interested in the dance but in the

Tommy Bell and his band not only provided music for many years at the Roxy Ballroom but some of the bandsmen went on to form their own groups to accommodate the need for dance music at the many small venues throughout East Northumberland.

music they knew."John, a pianist, said those self-taught then taught others and as a result the gap was filled. But, he pointed out, in the early stages of their careers they played second sax in the band where their contribution was generally only three notes.

He recalled one trainee sax player who knew only two tunes which he would play in the first half of the dance then leave the stage only to return after the interval to play them again. "It was learning on the job," said John.

While reed players were in short supply it certainly did not apply to pianists. There were at least six teachers in Blyth turning them out, one of the leaders in the field was Bobby Hindmarsh who taught at his home in Middleton Street. On one occasion he had 14 entrants in the North of England music festival and four were finalists.

Among those he took under his wing were Brian Lambert, later to become founder and conductor of the Blyth Orchestra, which is still in existence, and the Blyth Operatic Society orchestra and Elsie Tunney who qualified as an LRAM and was a leading light in the Wansbeck Music Festival where a trophy bearing her name is played for every year. Other notable personalities in the town who went on to tinkle the ivories very proficiently by courtesy of Mr. Hindmarsh were Freddie and Queenie Fordyce and Dr. Reg Carr.

The majority of big band players were supplied by the brass bands in the county. Here in Blyth it was the Cowpen and Crofton and L.N.E.R. bands who answered the dance bands need.

Stories of dance band times proliferate and John Stenhouse tells of one Blyth double bass player, Stan Parks, who owned a tiny Austin Seven car. He did not have a roof rack and the instrument was precariously fastened on the top. As he was driving to a dance the ropes fastened to the small side lamps on the bonnet snapped. Glancing through his rear mirror he saw to

The Kevin McLoughlin Band was resident at the St. Cuthberts Dance Club based at the church hall in Blyth. Kevin on accordion, Jack Stowell (guitar), John Stenhouse (piano) and Alan Nesbit (drums).

his horror his double bass bouncing along the road with pieces falling off.

John Stenhouse said: "He told us when he picked it up by the neck it looked like a scrawny chicken."

Stan, however, was a very skilled carpenter and spent hours repairing the instrument telling everyone afterwards: "It sounds even better than it did before the accident."
He did the job so well that he was able to sell the instrument on his retirement from playing.

Another recollection John has concerned Bill McCabe, a porter at the Thomas Knight Memorial Hospital who played the trombone. The night before the Northumberland Miners Picnic at Morpeth he got a call from the Cowpen and Crofton band asking if he could stand in for their lead trombonist who had gone sick.

Bill agreed and without having rehearsed came home with the first prize as best instrumentalist – a great tribute to his playing ability.
Several years ago a former police inspector, Fred Moffatt, wrote and self published a book called "Dance Hall Days" in which he looked at the dance bands and dance hall which proliferated at one time in the North East.

In the chapter on Blyth he traces the start of organised music in the town to the Blyth Symphony Orchestra and the Blyth Co-op Orchestra neither of whom catered for dancing. But it was those orchestras and the pit bands at the cinemas which could supply musicians who became dance band players.

The first dance hall, says Fred, was probably the Granthams Assembly Rooms by the Quayside but this later became the Gaiety Theatre of Variety.

He goes on: "One provider of players was the orchestra of the old Empire in Beaconsfield Street in which Leslie Bridgewater, later to become nationally famous, was a leading light (see Tommy Bell, Personalities of Blyth). Many of the players went on to big bands."

It was the arrival of Bill Tudor, the great showman (he was featured in the Part Two edition of Blyth Memories) that brought regular organised dancing to the town. He built the Tudors Ballroom, later to be renamed the Roxy, alongside his Hippodrome Cinema.

Saturday nights at the Tudors were, however, the province initially of Jos. Q. Atkinson, a Blyth man, who carved a great reputation throughout the North East with his band. He later established a dance band agency in Newcastle and was able to provide bands for every occasion.

When Jos Q. finished at the Tudors Tommy Bell took over and included in his line-up were Ted Durrant, later to play for the famous Squadronnaires band, Bob Thompson, Ted Barker and Eddie Watson.

Eddie not only played for Tommy Bell but he also turned out for local bands at the South Blyth Band Room, Cowpen and Crofton Welfare and Bebside Memorial Hall, where Harry Hogarth had his band. The Embassy Five, the Mal Armstrong Five and the Eric Agnew Band also played there and another, much later, which became extremely popular was led by Alistair Atkinson.

Back to the dance halls, and the Tudors did not have its own way in the Blyth. In the 1930's the Old Assembly Rooms on the Quayside were refurbished and dancing restarted with music provided by Raymond Hall and his Orchestra. Unfortunately the building caught fire and was completely destroyed.

It would certainly have thrived had it been operating at the outbreak of war. The Tudors, now known as the Roxy under the ownership of Sol Sheckman, was extremely busy catering for the hundreds of servicemen posted to the town. Blyth was the second largest submarine depot in the country and the sailors, along with a smaller number of airmen and soldiers, needed entertainment.

Even after the war ended and the troops dispersed dancing continued to be popular six nights a week at the Roxy. The management even had a professional dancer to provide lessons some evenings and on a Saturday afternoon. The tuition, and the dancing ended in the early sixties as rock and roll took over.

There are no regular dances in Blyth nowadays but there is still the fifteen piece Bebside Big Band which rehearses and plays for dances in the town. It also travels outside the town for engagements.

Whose to say with the popularity of the dancing programmes on television that the era of dancing to the big band won't return?

The Mal Armstrong Five. Mal on saxophone, Gerald O'Connell (bass), Les Stevenson (guitar), John Stenhouse (piano) and Ivan Barrass (drums). Apart from playing at local dances the group was also the resident band at the Queens Hotel in Morpeth.

Blyth's Golden Age of Youth Clubs

The Blyth boxing film which went around the country, the leader who called his members "scruffs and vagabonds" and wanted hippies to join and the youth club which doubled a church attendance. Just some of the anecdotes from the time Blyth boasted the Boys Club, YMCA and Methodist Youth Club and Centre 64.

Central Methodist Youth Club
by Gordon Young (Member 1959 to 1965)

The Central Methodist Youth Club based at the Central Methodist Church, alongside Post Office Square in Blyth, was the brain child of the Reverend Harry J. Blackmore, the Methodist minister, Mr. Blackmore decided he needed to encourage the youngsters of the town to become involved in the church and so formed the club Little did he know how successful it would become.

In 1959 the doors to the large school room attached to the church were opened on a Friday night and from an initial handful of teenagers the club grew into one the largest youth organisations in the North East, culminating in the building of the Centre 64. Teenagers travelled from Seghill, Seaton Delaval, Cramlington and Bedlington, as well as all parts of Blyth to enjoy the Friday night experience, which became popularly known as "The Meth"

Every Friday from 7.30 until 10.00 the hall would be packed with teenagers firstly playing table tennis, cards, chess, listening to music etc., or just catching up with friends, this was followed either with a film show or talk from local people on various subjects ranging from politics to rock and roll music.

The then Member of Parliament, Eddie Milne, was a regular visitor and many a good debate ensued. Mr. Bill Sullivan, local historian, and Squadron Leader James Rush, Second World War pilot and Newcastle United Director also came along together with the owner of the Record Bar in Bowes Street, Blyth, ("Badgy" Harrison) who gave an insight to the music industry and played the latest hits.

Gordon Young.

The club initially had a basic music system, a record player, but progressed to a state of the art two deck multi change, fade in fade out, DJ microphone and speaker system.

Little did we know then that one of our own would become a big influence in the music industry in just a few short years. Tim Blackmore, the son of the minister, eventually became the first music producer on B.B.C. Radio One. He is now an executive with the Sony Music Corporation as well as the owner of two radio stations.

The final session of the night was the dance. In the early days the Dashing White Sergeant and Strip The Willow were popular but very soon only the latest hits were played, except, however, for the last dance of the night, the Bradford Barn. Then you could dance with almost everyone of the opposite sex in the room, passing from one partner to the next and hopefully ending with the one you fancied asking for a date.

During the breaks for each session of the night it was not unusual to find the back yard to the church hall crowded with all the boys puffing away on cheap Woodbine or Nelson cigarettes, and the girls in a side anti room fixing their make up.

Occasionally dances were held on Saturday nights with either a local up and coming group providing the entertainment or a fancy dress theme being the order of the day almost all members turning out in style.

Each year the club would put on a variety show, The Mirthquake, with all members taking some part, be it in a pantomime sketch, a song or dance, or imitating favourite artist of the day.

In 1962 the club, in conjunction with the church, held a Freedom From Hunger campaign, to highlight the plight of the children in the Africa as part of a United Nations campaign. The front of the church was covered with posters, banners and photographs highlighting the plight of the children in many parts of the vast continent.

Leaflets were distributed throughout the town and an information centre set up within the entrance to the church. Bread and cheese lunches were also held in the school hall. The event brought to the attention of the people of Blyth, for what may have been the first time, the suffering of people from other countries.

The members provided their own disco music and were delighted when a new sound system arrived at the club. Keeping an eye on it are Gordon Young (left) and John Wilson, the d.j.'s at that particular disco session.

The club membership was at its peak during the music explosion of the Mersey Beat, and on at least two occasions a bus load of members went to the City Hall in Newcastle to see the Beatles, courtesy of one of the members, Joan Bradley, who stood in long queues for many hours to purchase tickets for everyone.

Otterburn Hall was a venue used by the club for weekends designed for Christian fellowship, with an annual visit around Easter time. London was also on the itinerary with again annual visits to the Methodist Association of Youth Clubs (MAYC) weekends, where clubs from around the country would meet, with events taking place in the Central Methodist Hall and the very grand Royal Albert Hall. Members would either stay in the homes of other club members in the London area or in youth hostel type accommodation in the area. Through events like these the club was to establish links with similar clubs in the region with exchange visits taking place with clubs along the Tyne Valley and Penrith.

Many friendships and marriages honed at the club have lasted the test of time. This was evident when Peter Endean, John Keenleyside and I organised a reunion in 1989 at Blyth Sports Centre. Over 200 former members turned up, some travelling from far flung parts of the globe, just to renew old friendships.

The Reverend Blackmore's plan certainly succeeded for attendances at Sunday evening service was doubled by club members who filled the balcony area of the church for quite a few years.

Throughout the years help was provided by Ron Charlton, Gordon Daley, Brenda Lambert and Marjorie Fraser who, although having supervisory roles, more than enjoyed themselves also as members.

The club saw a change in the mid sixties when members moved into their late teens or early twenties and being involved with pressures of work and family commitments.

However the new club, Centre 64, was born and a new era of the "METH" began.

Rev. Harry T. Blackmore.

The Birth of Centre 64

It was a government decision which led to the establishment of Centre 64 with a fulltime leader and assistants. The Albermarle Report recommended money be ploughed into the setting up of organisations to develop specialist and permanent places for youth to meet and learn.

Thanks to the efforts of Brian English, the Blyth optician, and other members of the church trustees the church was granted the funds to develop it further. It meant that a professional leader could be appointed and the position went to Fred Doyle a Yorkshireman who spent almost four years in the town.

A storehouse owned by the church but being used by Bulmans, the fruit and vegetable merchants, was taken over and then demolished to make way for a two-storeyed building attached to the rear of the church.

The new youth club, as the title suggests, was opened in 1964 to both boys and girls which was unusual in those days. The Boys Club and YMCA were boys only but followed suit – not entirely successfully. Ron Charlton was appointed full time leader and he was assisted in the kitchens by ladies of the church. One of them was Mrs Edna Charlton, now an 88-year-old widow living in North Farm.

She was eventually appointed a paid assistant leader and accompanied parties of the club members from the church to places of interest around the region and further afield. She tells how on one occasion she was in a van supporting eight club members – four boys and four girls – on a sponsored cycle ride to London.

Fred Doyle – the first full time professional leader of Centre 64

"We used to feed them by cooking in the van and we were shocked to learn afterwards that it was illegal to do that as anything could have happened."

Edna also recalls when she and her fellow helper, Ann Taylor, later to marry the club leader Colin Bullarwell, needed the toilet urgently. "We had stopped outside London and there wasn't one in sight so we hopped on the tandem and set off on the hunt. After travelling a fair while we couldn't find one as it was open countryside. Without going into detail we returned back in good order."

A highlight of the year was the annual trip to London to join up with representatives of other Methodist youth organisation at the Albert Hall. Up to 50 members travelled in a T & B bus driven many times by George Hudson – a hero of the town. He was badly burned trying to extinguish a blazing motor cycle in Waterloo Road.

On the sporting front the Centre Sixty Four football team was coached by Norman Penrose who had played for Newcastle United and Blyth Spartans and was now living in the town. And it was him who spotted the talent of Fred Turnbull and recommended him to Aston Villa whom he served with distinction until injured at the age of 28. The selling of the church to the Mall developers signalled the end of the youth club.

Blyth Town Boys Club

Blyth Town Boys Club started life in the third floor of the Arcade building in Waterloo Road which later became a café then a Chinese restaurant. As it developed it moved to the Irish club in Wright Street and eventually across the road to the former Wright Street Infants School.

Under the auspices of Charlie Mills and then Jack Allen the reputation of the club spread throughout the country because of the innovations they introduced. These included silk screen printing, a club newspaper, soccer, cricket and boxing.

It was in boxing that the fame of the club was spread throughout the National Association of Boys club because of a black and white film made by two of the members.

Jack Allen, a long serving leader of the Boys Club.

It featured a boxing match between "Punchy" Nichols from Cambois, the champion of British Rail and George Downey, a miner and a member of the club.

George, now 89, recalls: "I was a pretty well made lad and had boxed in the Royal Navy and Charlie asked me to be the opponent to the champion.

"The two lads filmed us as if it were a real boxing match with Jack Allen, who took over from Charlie when he left for the YMCA, as the referee. I remember hitting the champion on the nose with a straight left which I knew had hurt him.

"It was a bit of a mistake because he really let loose and his me with an uppercut which sat me on my backside. I tried to get up but my legs wouldn't move."

This short film was shown in boys clubs throughout Britain and got Blyth a deserved reputation as a go-ahead club not only for the boxing but also the filmed scenes of other activities at Blyth.

During its life the Blyth club was visited by a staunch supporter and former member of the National Association of Boys Club, Frankie Vaughhan. The singer, who had also starred in a Hollywood film with Marilyn Monroe, compered a concert of local performers in aid of the association at the old Newlands School which was on the site of the present Bede Academy in the Avenues.

The first leader of the Blyth Boys Club which was formed in was Ogilvie. He was followed by Charlie Mills and then Jack Allen.

George Downey (left), Jack Allen (referee) and "Punchy" Nichols, British Rail boxing champion from Cambois, before the bout.

Attending the official opening of the Blyth Town Boys club building just before the outbreak of the Second World War were (left to right) Johnny Adams, Bob Laws, Stan Parker, Ted Roberts and Johnny Stenhouse.

Blyth YMCA

Blyth YMCA began life in the Central Buildings, later to become the Central cinema, in 1891 when 30 young men attended the inaugural meeting. It then led a chequered existence in Soulsby's butchers shop in the Market Place, the Missions to Seamen, then a wooden hut in the Bus Station square.

The hut had been provided free of charge by Blyth Urban Council on the understanding it would be removed and the site restored once a more permanent home could be found. The hut, incidentally was moved to the 12 hole Blyth Golf Course where it became the clubhouse.

It was in 1925 the YMCA got a solid, permanent home, which was its headquarters until they went out of existence more than 60 years later.

Croft House in Waterloo Road had been the residence of the Keenlyside family, one of the leading ships chandlers in the town. It was bought for the YMCA and officially opened on Friday, March 20 th., 1925, by Mr. Angus Watson of Newcastle, a leading spiritual and moral philanthropist.

Councillor William C. Robson then presented Mr. Watson with a souvenir key. The life of the YM moved on steadily until the arrival of a leader called Eryl Davies whose style of management caused ructions. In 1966 he wanted to invite "hippies" to the club, went public with allegations against the morals of the youngsters in the area and called members "scruffs and vagabonds".

He proved to be the last full time leader at Blyth for when he left for Glasgow his job was taken on a part-time and temporary basis by Gerry Evans, a credit controller at Fergusons Transport. The "temporary" basis lasted 28 years

Looking back, Gerry who had gained experience as an assistant to the Blyth Town Boys Club leader, says: "Things at the YM were at rock bottom with memberships down to a handful and the building in Waterloo road almost derelict.

"It took me some time, with a lot of help and support from successive presidents, Bart Kinnair and Bill Elliott,, to get the building repaired, altered and revamped. Membership quickly grew and eventually the association had between eighty and one hundred youngsters there."

Recalling the problems he had because of the previous leader Gerry says: "An example of the attitude of the previous leader is illustrated when a well-known Blyth policeman, Jim Marnock, was asked to remove his helmet by the leader on entering the building with the aggressive words 'You would take your hat off when going into any other house'.

Eryl Davies, whose tenure as leader of Blyth YMCA was "rather unusual".

"Some years later when Mr. Davies paid a visit to Blyth and entered the club I ordered him out. I just could not stand him being there after what he had done. When he refused I rang Jim Marnock and he was only too happy to come and do the job – and he was wearing his hat."

A lot of the success of his time at the club stems from the fact that the Womens Auxillary, ably led by Mrs. Jane Gurney, constantly used and supported the club with money raising efforts.

Sport was also a key factor in the success of the club with table tennis, snooker, football and cricket. On the table tennis side they boasted the England seventh-ranked player, Peter Hoyles

One of the highlights of his term came In 1973 when thirty members travelled from Blyth to Norway to meet members of the KFUM – the foreign equivalent of the YM. For many it was their first time out of the town.

For his work at the YMCA Gerry was made Rotary Citizen of the Year in 1989 – seven years before he retired at the age of 65.

Although the Blyth club was turned over to be run by the North East Federation of YMCAs it was eventually closed down through lack of membership in 1998.

Although the Blyth YMCA closed in 1998 the sign still remains on the building which is used for several activities including a dance school.

The Ferry Across the Water

The time when a million and a half passengers were ferried across the River Blyth in a year; a ferryman who saved a man with a boy on his shoulders and a knight of the realm who helped stop fare dodging on the ferry. All tales from the fascinating history of the Blyth High Ferry.

The need to have assistance to cross the river started in the late fifteenth century when travellers could either wade through at low tide or pay the ferrymen who ran privately operated rowing boats.

There was a wooden structure about 20 feet in length alongside the Bucks Hill ford which could also be used at low tide to cross but it was completely submerged at half tide.

In 1859 the Blyth Harbour and Docks Company, which controlled the harbour, sought to take over and regulate the ferries and applied successfully to purchase one from its owner, Sir Matthew Ridley. Fourteen years later the Company took over all the rowing boats operating as ferries on the river. By this time one of them was large enough to carry a horse and cart. One year later a major incident occurred when a man who had been delivering goods by horse and cart to Cambois decided to use the Bucks Hill ford on his return journey instead of travelling to East Sleekburn to use the more popular and safe one. Unfortunately the cart stuck in the river bed and as the tide came in it threatened to drown the man and his boy assistant. Placing the boy on his shoulders they both started to shouting for help. Their cries were heard by one of the ferryman and he rowed to their rescue. The horse, however, was drowned. The incident caused an outcry and a demand from people north and south of the river for a bridge to be built. It was to be the first of many unsuccessful appeals for a more substantial means of crossing the river.

Passengers stood in the open on the early ferries while the engine and boiler were housed in the two huts either side of the vessel. To the right of the picture can be seen the second ferry which was used in tandem but also as a replacement should there be a breakdown.

There was a wooden rail bridge at Bebside but it was 1961 before a road bridge and pedestrian way was opened alongside it.

Blyth Harbour Commission was formed in 1892 and took over the Harbour and Docks Company the duties including the running of the ferries. It soon sought to improve the service and accepted a tender from the Union Co-operative Shipbuilding Company, which operated from what is now known as Ritsons Jetty, for a steam driven, large vessel to be pulled across the river by a winch engine.

Wires would be attached to both sides of the river and passed through the top of two legs in the middle of the vessel passengers would stand in the open with the only cover housing the engine room and boiler. This ferry which came into operation a couple of years laterwas not without its troubles – mainly caused by the crew. Mr. John Easton, who ran the Ridley Estates office which rented the ferrying rights to the Harbour Commission and took five eighths of any profits, informed Sir Matthew Ridley that he had received "strong and persistent" agitation for a more efficient ferry service. He had letters of complaints alleging delays and danger from Blyth and Cowpen town councils, Cowpen Coal Company and residents of Cambois.

He told the knight: "Unfortunately the ferrymen have not been strictly carrying out their instructions and probably, largely owing to their laxity, the ferry service has got disorganised somewhat and will required to be regulated afresh."

One allegation against the crew, apart from operating an irregular service, was that one man who collected the fares had been giving large discounts to one family. Sir Matthew took up the problem with the Commission which led to pay booths being established on both sides of the river and a tightening of discipline. The rumblings for a bridge surfaced again in the years after 1890 and pressure was put on the Commission to consider a swing bridge and indeed plans were produced. It was to have two spans, each over 100 feet in length, but after lengthy discussions the Commission engineers recommended that because of the high winds and rough weather during the winter months, it should be built higher up the river.

The first steam driven ferry between Blyth and North Blyth.

In the meantime, while consideration was being given for the bridge, an order was placed with the Blyth Dry Docks and Shipbuilding Company for a replacement ferry. This vessel would have passenger saloons on each side with the centre kept open for horses and carts. As far as the bridge plan was concerned it was abandoned in 1903 because of its vast expense - £40,000 for the bridge which did not included the cost of the approaches. One year later the new ferry came into operation using an engine which had been built by Hawthorn Leslies of Newcastle originally for a trawler. It could carry 300 passengers and two horse and carts. It was tested successfully, fortunately for the 800 boys who were packed on board on its first trip. It operated on alternative trips with the older vessel which continued in service until after the First World War when it was replaced by a twin of the 1904 model.

The most modern of the ferries with passenger rooms on either side and space for three cars.

The two ferries operated night and day together for over fifty years with the peak time being in 1946 when it was reported they had been used by one and a half million passengers and 30,000 vehicles in the twelve months. Its success was not continued for within twenty years, in 1964, the Commission closed the ferries citing economic reasons, it had lost money on the ferries over the previous ten years, and because of the popularity of the new Bebside road bridge. In addition the Northumberland County Council, Blyth Borough Council and Wansbeck Urban Council had withdrawn subsidies amounting to £22,000.

A full load of cars, bicycles and passengers disembark from the High Ferry in the 1950's.

The last ferry to operate on the river Blyth was this motor launch – obviously available to passengers only.

The boats were replaced by two passenger only motor ferries, each capable of carrying 100 passengers, which started a service between Blyth, North Blyth and Cambois which also served the Power Station. One was withdrawn in 1967 and the second in 1997. The Harbour Commission took the action as it felt other economies were needed because of the demolition of houses at Cambois, the fall off of coal shipments from the North Blyth staithes and the transfer of the British Rail Depot from the north side of the river. One of these vessels continued its ferrying career on the River Trent while the other was used as a general purpose launch by the Harbour Commission. And so after 130 years ferries across the River Blyth came to an end.

All trace of the Blyth Chain Ferry has vanished. The metal structure in the foreground was built after it closed and leads to a series of wooden steps down to a small landing used by the passenger only ferry which replaced the original.

Blyth's Olympic Boxing Coach

A Blyth miner who became an Olympic boxing coach, who was arrested for ferreting at Lambton Lion Park and who turned down the chance to be a professional boxer, just part of the life story of 78 year old Bill Craigs.

The Craigs family into which Bill was born in 1934 in Bebside was Jimmy and Alice, and their three daughters, Elsie, Margaret and Isobel. The arrival of Bill, the only boy, was well welcomed by sports loving Jim who, when the lad was still at school encouraged him to take up boxing.

Jim, a miner at Bebside Pit, who was also manager of the Bebside Gordons football team, was a keen boxing enthusiast and decided he himself would coach Bill at the local centre for the sport, the Bebside Welfare Memorial Club.

Bill later started work in the mines - a career which took him to Bebside, Bates, Netherton and Brenkley collieries – less nine years out as an able seaman in the Royal Navy.

Jim's coaching, however, was so successful that Bill won the Northumberland and Durham NCB light welterweight title and reached the quarter finals of the national championships.

One of the coaches who helped train Bill at Choppington for those championships was Chris Praill, a heavyweight who, during his career as Chris Rock, fought and lost to the famous Jack London. Boyed by this success Jim took his son to St. James' Hall, Newcastle, the mecca of boxing in the region to watch several professional bouts with a view to him joining the moneyed ranks.

Bill Craggs in boxing pose when a youngster.

"My Dad wanted me to fight under the name of Billy Luke – Luke being the Christian name of my two grandfathers. But things became rather strained between us when I told him I felt I was not mature enough to become pro and did not want to do it. That was when we fell out.

"We did not exactly stop speaking but after this I packed in boxing completely and gave all my gear, boots, shorts and tops to a friend who, fortunately, as it later turned out did not box and kept them safe."

But Bill was not short of hobbies, he kept pigeons and was also a great ferret man regularly going out hunting rabbits. At one time he and his mate, Eddie Morton, had the ferreting rights all around the town of Wooler. But there was one section around the town they did not have the rights and it led to a confrontation with the farmer who owned the land.

They had travelled to the field on their motor bikes and on returning after ferreting found the tyres on both bikes had been let down.

The farmer approached and said he had done to which Eddie Morton grabbed him and pushed him down near the wheel and said: "Then you'll blow them up yourself."

On one occasion Bill and another friend, Wilf Cape, headed for North Durham and a spot of ferreting after a friend told him where there were hundreds of rabbits. They were busy working their pets even though they could hearing lions roaring and see vehicles painted like zebras on the brow of a hill.

Just a few of the medals Bill was presented with at tournaments where his boxers were successful.

Before they knew it they were surround by uniformed men and told they were trespassing in Lambton Lion Park. Their excursion near the wild beasts cost them each £20 at the local magistrates court.

"It was and expensive trip. At first the magistrates were talking about us facing fines of £100 each. Even £20 was a lot of money in those days. Mind you I don't know if we were within eating distance of the lions. There appeared to be some kind of fence there but we never really thought about it although we could hear the loud roars."

Five years after quitting boxing Bill enlisted in the Royal Navy where there were various sports on offer. His boxing prowess soon brought him into contact with the gymnasium boxing ring and gave him full confidence to take up the gloves again. But before he did so he had to write to his friend to ask if he still had his gear and if he had, could he send it.

"Fortunately he had looked after it and while wearing some of that gear I went on to win the 1966-67 Far East Inter Service light heavyweight championship at the age of 32 and that, as it ultimately turned out, proved to be the last time I fought."

Bill served nine years in the navy, mainly in the Far East, but on returning to Bebside and work in the mines, quit boxing and started on what was to turn out to be a highly successful coaching career a career started by an incident involving one of his two stepsons, Larry French.

Bill said: "The lad came in crying one night and I asked him what was up. He said he had been training at a boxing gym in Ashington without me knowing and had been beaten in a local schoolboys final. I asked him how many fights he had had and he said that was the only one. "I told him straight away he was not going back to that club anymore. I was so incensed at him being so unprepared for a maiden fight that I took him down to the Blyth Town Boys Club where Laurie Hepples and George Fulcher coached and began helping out there. With good training, he came on so much that he reached the final of the All England Schoolboys national competition where he was beaten on points."

Although he was not to know it at the time Bill was starting on a career which would lead to him helping to train the British Olympic squad for three Olympics. It came about because Laurie Hepples assisted the England coach, Ian Irving, to train Olympic hopefuls in the North East at schoolboy, intermediate and senior level.

Bill in his England track suit.

"Eventually I got involved in this training and then went on courses over two years where I obtained my assistant, full coach, senior and advanced qualifications," said Bill. "With those I got into the England set up at Crystal Palace and I'm eternally grateful for the financial help I got in having to travel to London particularly from the committee of the Blyth Boys Club."

Among the internationals Bill help train were Audley Harrison and Richie Woodhorn who took gold and bronze at the Sidney Olympics. He also helped train the famous North East heavyweight Manny Burgo who was just beaten in the NBA semi final by the man who went on to win the title.

In all Bill help train boxers who competed also in Athens and Atlanta Olympics. Bill eventually became so proficient he qualified to coach coaches and made regular trips to venues between the Scottish Borders and Leeds to carry out examinations and practices. Bill, on leaving the Blyth Town Boys Club, helped establish boxing clubs at Newbiggin and Bedlington Station before eventually retiring from the sport in 1999 at the age of 64.

At his home in Ravensdale Close, Cowpen Estate, he reckons he had eighty fights in his career. Asked how many he had won he says: "Oh, I can't remember." Then how many did he lose? With a smile: "Not many."

Blyth at War – Part Two
Battle in the Air

Although I was born and lived throughout the Second World War in Blyth I was astonished when I came across a diary which included a large number of incidents involving bombings and air fights in the area. Note how the number of incidents declined as the war progressed and the Allies got the upper hand.

1940
Monday, April 29th. Sgt. Collyer killed in his Spitfire off Blyth. His body was recovered from the North Sea.
Tuesday, May 2nd. Shipping attacked in River Blyth by German aircraft approximately 600 yards up the river.
Thursday, June 27th. German plane crashed three miles east of Blyth. After a search by the coastguard nothing was found. The mine it dropped was 300 yards east of Blyth Pier.
Saturday, June 29th. German flying boat dropped a mine near the West Staithes. The mine exploded and windows of some houses half a mile away were blown out.
Monday, Sept 2nd. South Harbour Prop Yard and Newsham North Farm were bombed.
Tuesday, Sept 3rd. Eight bombs dropped on Blyth fields. Three rabbits and one peewit were killed.
Thursday, November 14th. Mines laid in North Sea off Blyth.

Many bodies were washed up at Blyth during the early part of the war – merchant seamen, sailors and airmen. The bodies of four Merchant Navy men were found on the foreshore in May, 1940, and were unable to be identified. They were buried alongside each other at the Links Cemetery, Blyth, the cost being born by the local authority. The inscription on the graves reads under a large M.N. "A sailor of the 1939-45 war. Merchant Navy. Buried 18th March, 1940." The bodies of German flyers which drifted ashore were transferred to Chevington Cemetery where they were interred in a special plot.

1941
Saturday, February 15th. Twelve houses in Blyth and Newsham were bombed and twelve people injured. Sgt. Brandon shot down a German aircraft four miles of Blyth. New Delaval Pit at Newsham near railway line bombed.
Sunday, February 16th. East of Newsham Railway Station and Gloucester Lodge Farm bombed, Rocks off Blyth bombed. South View at Newsham bombed.
Monday, February 24th. A bomb dropped by a German plane killed Elizabeth Moody of 34, Percy Street, Blyth.
Monday, March 4th. Cowpen was bombed by high explosives. St.Cuthbert's R.C. Church and a garden were damaged.
Saturday, March 8th. Horton Grange Farm bombed.
Monday, April 7th. Two high explosives fell on North Farm, Bebside. Craters were 60 feet wide and six feet deep.

Wednesday, April 16th. Blyth was bombed. Blyth Railway Station signal box was bombed by parachute. Signalman killed.
June, 1941. The King and Queen visited Blyth. Children from some of the schools were waiting in Park Road and Beaconsfield Street to see them pass by as they headed for Blyth Shipyard after visiting the South Harbour and the Naval base.
Thursday, August 7th. Air duel over the Blyth Coastguard station lookout at South Harbour. Stray bullet went through a window.
Saturday, August 9th. RAF Whitley bomber crashed in the North Sea 78 miles off Blyth.
Thursday, October 2nd. A German Dornier shot down six miles off Blyth. Three rescued from plane. Four months later on Sunday, February 15th, another Dornier was shot down four miles off Blyth. On this occasion no one in the crew survived.
Friday, November 7th. Bombs dropped in the River Blyth. Houses and windows damaged.

1942
Sunday, February 15th. A Dornier was shot down four miles off Blyth in the North Sea. No survivors.

A Dornier bomber similar to this one was shot down on Thursday, October the 7th, 1941, off Blyth. Three of the four man crew were rescued.

Friday, May 5th. Robert Watson, skipper of the fishing boat Dagney picked a Dornier 217 engine in his net.
Sunday, May 24th. RAF Spitfire attacked German aircraft south of Blyth.
Monday, June 2nd. German Heinkel 115 crashed one mile off Blyth after flying up and down the river. Believed to be hit by ack ack. One mine had been dropped.
Sunday, June 7th. RAF Spitfire crashed in the North Sea, north east of Blyth. Pilot killed.
September 15th. Ack ack fire brought down a German aircraft four miles off Blyth.

1943
Thursday, March 11th. RAF Beaufighter shot down German aircraft off Blyth.
Sunday, March 14th. RAF Beaufighter shot down a Junkers 88 off Blyth. One body found and brought back to Blyth.
Saturday, September 4th. RAF Lancaster M111 crashed 15 miles off Blyth in the North Sea.

1944
Thursday, August 8th. A United States Army Air Force B17G aircraft crashed in the North Sea off Blyth.

All these incidents of the Second World War in and off Blyth were recorded only in official records. Security was tight as it was forbidden to keep pictures and information privately in case it fell into enemy hands. Even members of the Home Guard fell under the restriction. However, after the war, an individual known only as A. Conway apparently collated the above for posterity and for this we are grateful.

The work of the Air Raid Precaution wardens during the five years of war was important but became spasmodic for as the conflict progressed the number of times the warning siren could be heard dwindled. The wardens proudly marched through the town as part of the 1945 Victory Parade.

The Rise and Fall of the Singing Miners
by Dorothy Hartshorne

It was 1921 at a time of great depression and unemployment in the mines that a notice was put up on the Bebside pit heap inviting anyone interested in singing to attend a meeting at the Mechanics Institute. It was signed "Music Lover". It led to the formation of a choir which over the next 50 years swept the board at singing competitions up and down the country.

Fifty three men, mostly miners, turned up at the Institute and voted for the formation of the Bebside Male Voice Choir on September 1st., 1921. One of them was William Bell, who became conductor, and the remaining 52 were all accepted in the choir. Three months later the choir gave the first of what turned out to be hundreds of concerts. It was held on December 28th in the Bebside Methodist Church Hall and tickets were sold at 1s.6p. and half price for seats at the back of the hall. Almost 120 tickets were sold and the choir made a profit of seven pounds. Six numbers were sung by the choir and several solos from guest artistes including Gladys Smith who was to become one of the finest music and singing teachers in East Northumberland.

The first accompanist was Annie Bainbridge and it is recorded in the minutes that a Mr. Bainbridge would be paid two shillings and sixpence a night for the hiring of the piano. One can only surmise the relationship — wife or daughter?

One Shilling

By now the rules had been laid with members paying a one shilling entry fee into the choir then three pence a fortnight dues. While most of the members could read music it was not essential. It was also agreed that members singing solos at concerts should be paid two shillings and sixpence for one song and five shillings for two

The choir rehearsed on a Thursday night at the Mechanics Institute and it is noted that as William Bell, the conductor, was a teetotaller "strong drink" was never allowed after practice or indeed at concerts.

Whether or not the discipline paid off is not known but they were much in demand for during the six years from 1924, apart from numerous concerts indoors for charity, including the Empire Cinema in Blyth and Bedlington Picture Palace, they also sang out of doors. They gave concerts in Carlisle Park, Morpeth, Bog Houses, Hartford, the Co-op Store field, Newsham, and Ridley Park, Blyth.

The choir also cleaned up at music festivals winning at the Wansbeck, Leeds and Sunderland events and flower shows at Felling, Prudhoe and Stamfordham.

By 1924 the popularity of the choir now meant that voice tests for new members were introduced. These took place in the front room of the conductor's house at Bebside. The success of the singers was such that in 1930 they were renamed the Bebside and District Prize Male Voice Choir. Their annual celebrity concerts were the most eagerly anticipated being given every February in the Central Cinema with Owen Brannigan a regular soloist.

Gladys Willis, the regional BBC accompanist, was the official accompanist for the annual concerts beginning a lifelong association with the choir. She became president many years later. During the first decade the choir's reputation had spread so far that international artistes from London, including Heddle Nash, Norman Allan, Constance Hay and May Huxley, sang with them.

Bebside & district Male Voice choir pictured after taking fourth place in the Blackpool Music Festival in 1919.

But the choir had to wait until 1938 for their first broadcast on the BBC in Newcastle. It was April 27th and they sang eight songs during the 40 minutes they were on the air on this occasion being accompanied by Kathleen Moorhead.

The outbreak of the Second World War saw the continuation of the celebrity concerts at the Central Cinema and the Wallaw at Bedlington Station although the choir numbers were much depleted through war service. Proceeds from the concerts, a total of £580 during the duration, were donated to the Blyth and Bedlington branches of the Red Cross. During the war years postal orders were sent off regularly to members of the choir serving in the forces and although there were some deaths many returned to find Billy Bell still the conductor and many founder members still singing.

In 1946 a Battle of Britain concert was given in the Theatre Royal, Blyth, and home coming concerts at Bebside and Choppington for Battle of Britain funds.

With the health of Billy Bell failing the conducting fell more and more on the shoulders of his deputy, Matt Hall, who took over on a permanent basis with the death of the first conductor.

Matt's sister, Nan, became accompanist in 1946 a position she held until her brother died. George Burlington then over as conductor and was waving the baton when the 50th Anniversary Celebration Concert was held in the Front Street Methodist Church, Bedlington, in 1971. It came less than 12 months after the entire music library of the choir, collected over almost fifty years, stored in the Bebside Memorial Hall was destroyed by fire which gutted the building.

By now the choir was down to 32 members but were still in great demand. A look through the minute book reveals the choir performing in churches and chapels in Blyth which are no longer in existence - the Regent Street Methodist Church, the Beaconsfield Street Primitive Methodist Church and the Weslyan Church. The choir was now rehearsing in the Front Street Methodist Chapel in Bedlington Station but the writing was on the wall as the membership further declined.

The last recorded celebrity concert of the choir, which had dropped the word "prize" from its title, took place in 1980 at the Blyth United Reformed Church. The guest artistes on that occasion were two professional singers from Blyth, both of whom were members of the church, Ann Guthrie and Kathleen Parker.

Although there is no official record of the choir folding it is believed it went out of existence during the eighties.

Bebside Memorial Hall fire which cost the choir its entire music library.

The Seven Stars Story

The first Seven Stars public house at North Blyth was built at Link End in the early part of the 18th century but was demolished in 1890 when the river was widened to allow bigger ships to enter the port. The landlord at the time, one William Christie, appeared in court during his tenancy for smuggling tobacco and gin and was fined.

A second Seven Stars was built towards the end of the Nineteenth century, this is the one Blyth folks still around can recall looking at across the river from the end of Bridge Street. Houses were built either side of it some years later.

The new Seven Stars was involved in several incidents. In January, 1913, the steamer Dunelm, from Sunderland, was wrecked off the East Pier. The Blyth Volunteer Life Saving Brigade helped in the rescue and survivors were given refuge in the Seven Stars. Unfortunately the second mate of the Dunelm died there. His was the second death in the incident as life saver George Hurrell, married with five children, died after working four hours in sleet and snow on the rocks.

The first Seven Stars public house was built in the 19th century but was demolished in 1890 when the river to be expanded to take bigger ships.

Mr. and Mrs. Allan, who ran the Seven Stars at the time, received a letter of thanks from one of the rescued seamen praising them for their help which including using almost every piece of clothing in the inn for the comfort of the rescued men.
Some 38 years later, in 1941, a strange incident happened when Rolf Halversen, a steward on board a Norwegian ship docked at Blyth, shot himself through the heart in the bar.

Mrs. Florence Olsen, the manageress, told an inquest the next day: "Mr. Halversen came in alone last night about eight o'clock. He ordered three whiskies but gave two of them away. He was quite sober and told me he was going out of this world and into the next.

"I jokingly said: 'I'll send you some flowers.' At which he laughed and said: 'I mean it. Tomorrow I will be a dead man'."

Mrs. Olsen said the man then left but returned after an hour and a half, spoke to his captain who was in the bar, then ordered a small whisky. "He started to write something in a little book," she said, "and then I heard the pistol go off. He had not drunk the whisky but as soon as I heard the bang I knew he had shot himself."
One month later, February, 1941, a high explosive bomb landed on the Target Rocks near Link end and damaged the pub.

The Seven Stars had a small jetty in front which was a highly popular spot for anglers who could leave their lines and pop in for a pint while waiting for a catch.

The pub, which operated throughout its lifetime using gas and later a generator for power, closed for good in 1967 and stood shuttered up until it, and the adjoining houses, were demolished in 1983.

The second Seven Stars was built towards the end of the 19th century, closed in 1967 and demolished 16 years later.

The Big Steeple Church

A minister who would follow any burial procession; a rebellion which split a church in two and the closure of the biggest landmark in Blyth which used to guide ships into harbour. Tales from the history of the United Reformed Church.

It took quite a while for religion to take a hold in Blyth but when it did it certainly took off with nine churches being built in just 15 years from 1861. The Methodists came first followed in successive years by the Roman Catholics, the United Presbyterians and St. Mary's Church of England. The Methodist New Connection was opened in 1867, the Congregationalists and Primitive Methodists in 1868 the Wesleyan Methodists in 1869 followed seven years later by the Waterloo Road Presbyterians.

It is a sad reflection on the trends of today as the only large religious buildings remaining in the town are St. Mary's, St. Cuthbert's, St. Wilfrid's and the Central Methodists. The Waterloo Road church, a Grade Two listed building, still exists but not for worship with the small congregation now using St. Wilfrid's Convent Chapel just across the road.

This is the story of the 130 year old United Reformed Church, the latest affected by dwindling congregations, we are telling, thanks to the invaluable help of Bill Thompson, the church historian. When it actually began in Blyth cannot be accurately dated although there are indications, although no direct evidence, that a rebellion by 2,000 ministers in 1662 over the Act of Uniformity led to them being expelled from the church.

They are then reported to have set up their own individual congregations. The Rev. Doctor Lomax of North Shields established teaching stations at North Shields and Old Hartley and, it is believed, a shared ministry with Blyth. If so it would indicate tenuously that it could be the oldest congregation in Blyth. The discovery of a communion plate marked 1777 certainly points to an existence from the 1770's.

United Reformed Church.

There are indications that the Rev. Thomas Craig, a schoolmaster and minister, led what was known as the Protestant Reformatory Congregation in prayers in a room above a rope warehouse in Queens Lane, near Ballast Hill.

It was there the Rev. Craig carried out the first baptism when he christened the son of one Thomas and Deborah Foreman in December, 1786. The minister also carried out teaching duties at the Reformed Church School but he seems to have left the town in 1790. He was not replaced until 1795 when the appropriately named Rev. John Blythe arrived.

The Rev. Blythe was a close acquaintance of the Delaval family and several letters from them were marked "Rev. Blythe of Blythe" – with Blyth and Blythe being accepted options at the time. The Minister is recorded as having carried out over 50 baptisms up to 1804.

It was the arrival of the Rev. William Robertson in 1807 at the start of a ministry lasting forty years that gave the church a boost. Known as "Priest Robertson" he was to lead the church away from the room over the rope warehouse to the first permanent home and school room for the church.

This was the Ebeneezer Chapel in Church Street, named from the words of an old hymn which included "safely to arrive at home." The new buildings cost £270 and in addition a manse for the minister was completed for £180

The Ebeneezer Chapel.

The Rev. Robertson was a kindly man but somewhat eccentric. His means of greeting was a tap on the shoulder with his walking stick. He is also recorded as joining any funeral procession he came across following at the rear of the mourners.

He was not, however, popular with everyone for his strange ways led in 1820 to a split in the church. His assistant, a Mr. Broadbent, led part of the congregation away and although Mr. Broadbent died suddenly the secessionists opened a "preaching station" in Crofton.

This group flourished, becoming known as the United Presbyterians and led by the first minister, the Rev. Daniel Carmichael. He was a powerful preacher and important figure in the town and was instrumental in having a new church built in Bridge Street in 1863. When it closed it was taken over as a pop factory.

In the meantime the Reformists continued under Priest Robertson and in 1831 joined the Presbyterian Synod of Northumberland which, five years later, linked with the Presbyterian Church of England. So now Blyth had two Presbyterian churches.

The Rev. John Reid became minister for the Reformist church in 1851 and under his ministry the congregation grew from 40 to 160 members completely outgrowing the Ebeneezer Chapel. A new building fund was established raising the amazing amount of £270 at that time from one bazaar alone.

The Rev. Reid moved on to work in Salford but plans for a new church at what was then the extreme western end of the town continued.

The church in Waterloo Road was officially opened on June 6th., 1876, the 200 foot high Gothic spire dominating the town and soon used by the local fishermen as a guide to port. It also boasted the highlight of the Victorian era – gas lighting.

The congregation was now facing a debt of £5,000, the cost of building the church, but within a year it had been halved although it took another 13 years before it was cleared completely.

The interior of the closed church with the giant organ in the background. Organist Dr. Reg Carr often plays it to keep it in tune.

The church, however, did not stop spending as the Ebeneezer chapel was now too small for a flourishing Sunday school so a hall was built in 1893 in Bondicar Terrace attached to the church at a cost of £1,270. Even more money was spent in paying £650 for the huge, magnificent, three manual organ built by Binns of Leeds in six months and installed by the same firm.

Many celebrated organists including the famous Sandy MacPherson of BBC fame gave recitals on the impressive instrument which had a fine reputation throughout the organ playing world.

The official closure of the United Reformed Church was marked with a Last Night at the Proms concert featuring mezzo soprano Alison Charlton, seen here with Dr. Reg Carr who accompanied singers on the huge church organ.

The church saw a victory party in January, 1919, for the returning soldiers but for 24 members of the church there was no return. Their names were engraved on a tablet by a memorial window.

The church expanded greatly between the wars with the church and gallery pews being packed for services and the Guides, Cubs and Scouts groups flourishing. A debating society and operatic society came into being.

The Second World War saw the church suffering damage from enemy action when a German land mile landed on the Blyth Station signal box killing the signalman and a local resident. A wagon wheel was blown the mile from the explosion to embed itself in the church spire.

And it was that same spire which cost the church £17,000 when it was found to have dangerous, severe internal decay in 1999. The supporting steel girder had to be replaced and this was followed by the replacement of stone window frames and repairs to the stained glass windows. With generous support from Blyth Valley Council and English Heritage the £18,000 cost was raised.

Earlier, in 1973, the Presbyterian church had joined with Baptists, Congregationalists and Churches of Christ to become the United Reformed Church. Unfortunately it did not halt the drop in attendances which left the church in 2008 with heavy financial commitments and only 46 members.

The minister, the Rev. Yvonne Tracey, consulted members and it was agreed to close the church and accept an offer from St. Wilfrid's to pray in the convent chapel, once used by nuns who lived in the large house adjoining the church.

It had been hoped weddings and funerals could be held in the old church but these will take place in the Central Methodist Church.

Since its closure there was a move to turn the church hall into a Maritime Museum but the idea was not progressed and the hall was then taken over in 2013 by the North East Music Factory to operate cheap activities to help the health of the local community.

Rev. Yvonne Tracey.

The Scottish Fisher Girls

A regular sight every summer behind Wensleydale Terrace in Blyth in the 19th and 20th centuries were the numerous fisher girls who followed the Scottish fishing fleets around the British coast chasing the shoals of herring.

The girls, who were employed by curers, were out in all weathers gutting, washing and cleaning the fish before packing them, sardine fashion, between layers of salt into barrels to await pickling and transportation, mainly to Germany, Russia and the Baltic states.

Up to 500 women and girls, mainly from the Scottish towns and villages, followed the fleet, sometimes 100 boats strong, from port to port during the herring season. They started on the west coast of Scotland in the early summer then moved down the east coast ending in Yarmouth and Lowestoft in the autumn.

The girls travelled by special trains and buses and slept where they could in lodging houses, camp sites and unfurnished wooden huts, if they were available. Because of the smell some lodging house keepers draped cloths on the walls of the rooms they rented to avoid the fish odour penetrating the buildings.

Though hard, it was a happy time for the lively, good-humoured and mainly attractive girls. The singing of Gaelic songs echoed throughout the trains and buses while woe betide any man who came within sight. He was met with a barrage of ragging.

The amount of herring landed at Blyth can be seen by the barrels in the background while interested youngsters watched the highly skilled fishergirls at work.

The girls worked in teams of three, two of them were gutters and the third, usually the tallest, was the packer. She packed the herring in tiers of salt in barrels.

The usual routine was the girls to be woken up, some of them sleeping three to a bed, early in the morning by a cooper with the call "get up and bandage your fingers." While having a cup of tea the girls would tie bandages around their fingers to avoid being nicked or cut with the sharp knives used to gut the herring. These were essential as the gutting was carried out very fast some 30 to 50 herring a minute, hour after hour, and the chances of cutting fingers was very high, particularly if they were distracted. Barrels of herring averaged 700 fish while the whole job of gutting, dousing and packing only took about ten minutes.

Work started at six in the morning and lasted until six in the evening but even longer if there was a glut of the fish. At half past eight the girls broke for a breakfast of porridge, bread and jam.

The gutting was done in a very quick movement with the gut removed with a twist of the hand. Without a glance from the girls, the fish, depending on their size, were thrown accurately, depending on the size – small, medium or large -into one of three containers on the floor behind them.

The small containers were then plunged into a pickling trough removed and then sprinkled with salt. Eventually the packer took over seizing handfuls of herring and arranging them in tiers in a rosette fashion, bellies uppermost and head facing the edge of the barrel.

They were again sprinkled with rough salt. After the fish had settled and the salt melted the barrels, which contained about 700 fish on average, were reopened and the pickle run off. They were once again filled to the top and resealed with a tight lid. They stood for ten days and the process repeated with fresh pickle poured in. Only after standing for a further fifteen days for maturing were they judged ready for export.

If the fishing was not so good they had reduced wages at the end of the season, sometimes just enough to cover pocket money. The average take home pay when the job was done was up to £12 for the season but the girls did not take poor pay lying down.

There was the occasional strike, one of them at Great Yarmouth when most girls stopped work seeking a rise of two pence – from 10 pence to 12 pence (one shilling) a barrel. Some of the older women were reluctant to come out and a large delegation of young girls was sent to get them to change their minds. This they did after being drenched with the powerful sea water hose.

The employers brought mounted police in to intimidate the girls but they continued the strike with good-humoured banter, singing and laughter. After a week they got their way and started working for one shilling a barrel.

A regular sight every summer behind Wensleydale Terrace in Blyth in the 19th and 20th centuries were the numerous fisher girls who followed the Scottish fishing fleets around the British coast chasing the shoals of herring. The Ridley Park hotel is in the background.

While the work of gutting the herring involved long hours of arduous and dirty work in poor conditions it had its compensations. The girls looked forward to the herring season each year as it was a lot of fun on Saturday nights especially when the boats were in port and the fishermen were able to attend the ceilidh. They always ended at ten o'clock as dancing and music was not allowed to run into the Sabbath.

Many of the girls met their future husbands at ports and sometime marriages took place, usually with someone from their home town, before they travelled back home.

The two world wars had a tremendous influence on the herring fishing industry with many of the girls committed to working in the munitions factories and nursing although many of them returned to fishing when the Great War ended.

Not many of the post war age group took up herring gutting as a career because of the depression while the men switched to the Merchant Navy. Attempts to revive it were also hit by countries launching their own fishing fleets and so the trade died out with the outbreak of the Second World War after being in existence For over 100 years.

Personalities of the Town of Blyth

Bill the All-Rounder

Possibly the most versatile person to ever come out of Blyth was a man whose life encompassed almost every facet of the town – cricket, table tennis, bowls, social work, magic, amateur dramatics, the Rotary movement and music. He was W.C. "Bill" Elliott whose contribution during the Second World War was to qualify as a pilot and then teach other airmen how to tow the gliders used in the attack on Arnhem.

On leaving Blyth Grammar School Bill was intent on a career in shipping in his booming home town port but instead enlisted in the RAF as aircrew at the outbreak of war. He soon began flying training which took him to Calgary in Canada for further instruction on Spitfires and where he eventually received his "wings". On his return to England he was awaiting a posting to Egypt but instead found himself switched to RAF Shebdon, Herefordshire, where he was to assist in the building and training of a glider force. Some of his trainees went on to tow the gliders used in the Arnhem landings.

It was while he was serving at RAF Sheldon that he met his future wife, Irene, who was working as a documents clerk at the station and was also a member, as was Bill, of the local amateur dramatic group. Although Irene was born in Lowestoft in Suffolk it was Blyth where they decided to live.

Back in civilian life Bill was accepted for teacher training but instead opted to join Northumberland Education Department as a clerk then moving on to the County Health Department as a mental health officer for Blyth. He was eventually appointed area director for social services in North Tyneside where he stayed until he retired in July, 1987.

Bill Elliot – Airman.

Throughout his working career and for a long time afterwards Bill involved himself in cricket with four clubs, Blyth, Blyth YMCA, Blyth Phoenix and Cambois Welfare. He told the tale of how he gave up playing the sport when, during a game, as he was chasing the ball towards the boundary he was overtaken by a youngster who shouted: "Don't bother, I'll get it."

Even after the insult he continued his association with the sport by becoming an umpire in the Northumberland League for 13 years.

He then took up bowls with the New Delaval club eventually becoming not only president of the Northumberland Federation but also the national president which saw him visiting many federations throughout England.

Bill received the highest award of the Rotary Movement – the Paul Harris Fellowship – for his distinguished 38 years service to the Blyth club as committee member, treasurer and president.

He was also treasurer of Blyth YMCA for nine years then chairman and eventually president. During his time there he also played table tennis where he was rated the number one player in the second team.

His involvement in amateur dramatics started with Blyth Phoenix, continued in the RAF, and led to him becoming a founder member, and vice president, of Blyth Valley Players.

Bill Elliott – Cricketer.

Throughout this part of his life he was involved in the production of 150 plays and pantomimes but still found time to play the flute and piccolo in augmented orchestras in Blyth, Ashington and North Shields. He was also an enthusiastic member of the Blyth Concert Orchestra formed by the late Brian Lambert.

Magic

As a member, and subsequently chairman of the Blyth Magic Circle he performed numerous shows for children.

As his wife Irene, now 90 and living in retirement in Blyth, says: "Bill was always active, here, there and everywhere. He certainly enjoyed life and it was a pleasure to share it."

W.C. "Bill" Elliot died on December 29th., 2005, at the age of 83.

Bill Elliott – President of English Bowling Federation.

Tommy Bell – Mr. Music

Blyth's "Mr. Music", as far as dance fame was concerned, was Tommy Bell. Born in the town in Old Nelson Place, now long disappeared, he studied the piano at the hands of Leslie Bridgewater, later to become famous nationally as a pianist, composer and conductor.

At the time Leslie was in charge of the orchestra at the Empire Theatre in Beaconsfield Street and it was there that Tommy started his musical career in the twenties.

He later formed a band with three of his cousins and played engagements at the Mechanic's Institute, which was later to become Blyth Library, and at the Grantham Assembly Rooms on Ballast Hill by the river.

Tommy Bell and his Rhythm Band soon became a twelve-piece and built a fine reputation throughout Northumberland.

It was in the thirties he was to start an association with the Tudors Ballroom, later to become the Roxy, which lasted three generations.

Called up to the RAF at the outbreak of war his band continued at the Roxy but eventually George Mason brought his band to Blyth from the Clayton Ballroom in Bedlington Station.

Tommy Bell.

Meanwhile Tommy was continuing his musical career playing in the Canal Area Orchestra which broadcast from Cairo and played for dancing at the exclusive French Club Ismalia in the city. He also entertained at many concerts for the troops stationed in the desert.

By now Tommy had become proficient on the saxophone and piano accordion and on his return from service duty persuaded Sol Sheckman, who had taken over the ballroom at the outbreak of war, to re-employ his band at the Roxy. So started an association which lasted until 1962 when rock and roll became the craze.

Tommy, a bachelor, retired to his home in Beaconsfield Street next to the Masonic Hall where he lived with his sister, Isabelle. He died in hospital in October, 1981, and was buried in Blyth Cemetery after a service attended by many former members of his band.

Leonora Rogers – Dancing Mistress

Leonora Rogers was the only daughter of Madam Rogers who ran a dancing school in Newcastle and other schools around the country. Leonora became such a proficient dancer she was able to become a professional. She appeared on stage around Britain in revues and pantomimes working for such impresarios as George Black, Jack Taylor, Ernie Hinge and Peter Davies.

During the war she joined ENSA – the group formed to provide entertainment for the troops – which took her into the war zones. After the war she moved to Blyth following her marriage to Jimmy Bell and they settled down in their home in First Avenue where she had three sons, Brian, Graham and Dennis.

Jimmy, later to become a town councillor, was a tenor and actively involved in the entertainment scene in the area.

Leonora decided to follow in her mother's steps and opened the Leonora Rogers School of Dance in St. Mary's Church Hall in 1947. It was an immediate success and her dancers performed at many charity concerts over the years. The major show, however, was the annual Battle of Britain Association Concert every September.

The reforming of the Blyth Amateur Operatic Society in 1959, in which Jimmy played a leading part, eventually led to Leonora being appointed choreographer taking some of her dance school pupils with her.

It was a position she held until her death in 1981.

Leonora Rogers in her professional dancing days.

Jimmy, who served as an independent on Blyth Borough Council for 13 years up to 1966, passed on in 2011 at the age of 92 spending his last years in the care home which now occupies the site of the former Thomas Knight Memorial Hospital in Beaconsfield Street.

Pauline Ryder – The Landlady

A pub landlady, a former model and beauty queen, who served free soup and beer to striking miners yet twice ejected some of them from the premises recalls her memories of running one of the liveliest bars in Blyth for over twenty years.

Seventy year old Pauline Ryder, now lives in retirement in Plessey Road with her husband Bob, 72, a former River Blyth pilot, almost opposite her former hostelry, the Joiners Arms.

Pauline was raised in the pub business through her family in the Durham area but worked as a model with the Louise James Agency in Newcastle before being spotted by an executive of the Sunday Mirror.

He offered her a job as Miss Lucy. She became one of the girls who toured holiday resorts wearing white dresses with a Miss Lucy sash.

If she saw anyone carrying a Sunday Mirror she approached them and asked them a question. One example being: "When was the Battle of Hastings." If she got the right answer she handed them a ten shilling note (fifty pence).

Her first solo venture in running a bar came when she took over a pub at Eighton Banks, Gateshead, and it was from there she moved to Blyth in 1977 to take over the Joiners Arms.

It was a popular meeting place for the striking miners in the eighties and their plight led to Pauline making soup in a huge gas boiler and serving it with a pint of beer free of charge.

"I really felt sorry for them," she said. "They had no money and were desperate. But mind you, there were some I did not take to."

When some miners broke the strike one of them came in to the Joiners. "This group in the corner threw him out of the pub for blacklegging so I barred them for doing it," she said. And she had to repeat the action some time later when what she called "the arrogant actions" of some of the miners still on strike upset regulars at the bar.

But Pauline was quick to praise other miners after the strike who had shown their gratitude for her hospitality during the stoppage. She told of how one former miner was years later working as a bouncer at a nightclub in Newcastle. "He recognized me straight away and allowed me and my friend in free of charge," she said.

She is fulsome in her praise for the local residents of Crofton for shortly after her arrival they were holding a street party for the Queens 25th Jubilee and made sure her five year old daughter, Anita, was invited and given a souvenir coin.

"I realised then the Blyth people were a bit special, they made us so welcome."

Another fond memory was when the Scots fishermen, who followed the shoals down the east coast, arrived in Blyth and settled on the Joiners Arms as their local. "I have never sold so much whisky in my life," she said. "They were great company."

Eyes Met

And someone else who turned out to be great company was Bob Ryder, who was a pilot on the River Blyth. Their eyes met across the bar, romance followed, and they eventually wed.

Bob spent most of his sea-going career as captain of ships ranging from a 250,000 oil tanker to colliers before taking the pilot's job at Blyth He spent sixteen years on the river before retiring.

The Joiners Arms soon developed into the place to go because of the wide and varied activities introduced by Pauline

Pauline Ryder – the happy landlady.

ably supported by regulars such as Bill Thompson, Bill Mitcheson and Peter Fraser.

Bill Thompson always opened the annual flower show by bringing in his giant sunflowers which were displayed at the front door while Peter Fraser was the champion chrysanthemum grower.

Apart from the flower show there was the annual tug of war, leek show, darts team, Easter Egg contest, quizzes and pony and trap meets. A number of Blyth men, led by local businessman Marshall Straughan, were pony and trap enthusiasts. They met regularly at the Joiners before setting off on a run and returned to a buffet laid on by Pauline.

"I think I left the pub trade at the right time," says Pauline. "The writing was on the wall but I certainly enjoyed my 20 years at the Joiners."

Hoot Gibson – Cowboy Copper

One of the best known policemen in Blyth between the First and Second world wars Fred Gibson who was known, but not to his face, as Hoot after the silent Hollywood screen cowboy hero, Hoot Gibson.

Before he started his 25 years in the Northumberland Police Force Fred served abroad with the 20th Battalion of the Northumberland Fusiliers and in 1916 was awarded the Military Medal for bravery in the field.

Before coming to Blyth he served as a police constable at Hexham, Seaton Delaval and Ashington and proved himself to be a fine sportsman winning many medals in police competitions. He spent most of his service in Blyth where he was noted for his fairness. On occasions, coming across a youngster doing wrong, Hoot would give the culprit a boot up his backside or a clip around the ear and a warning not to do it again.

Army Corporal Hoot Gibson.

He retired in 1944 from the force and eventually joined the National Coal Board as a security officer. Part of his duties was to accompany pay clerks to the local pits on a Friday when they carried large sums of money for the miners pay.

One pay clerk noticing Fred had a small, thick, black truncheon tucked in this belt and asked what it was and was told it had been used to kill a man.

Murder

Fred, in his police duties, attended a murder scene down by the river following a fight between two seamen. The truncheon, made out of lignum vitae, one of the hardest woods, was the murder weapon. Whether the killer was hung is not known but Fred purloined the weapon after the trial and kept it handy when escorting the thousands of pounds to the pits.

Fred spent ten years with the Coal Board before retiring to his home in Bohemia Terrace where he and wife Jean celebrated 50 years of marriage. Ten weeks later he died at the age of 72 and was cremated at Cowpen.

Hoot Gibson – a dandy.

Dorothy Hartshorne – Blyth's Bicycling Nurse

Dorothy Hartshorne, now 78, and an ex-Blyth Grammar School girl, started her working life as one of Hedley Young's "Little Ladies" – the name given to all the young female employees at the large store in the centre of Blyth. It was run on easier lines than at the local co-op where if a girl got married she had to leave their job.

"While it was strict but fair at Hedley's at least we could keep our work if we wed," she said.

But Dorothy fancied a career in nursing and while a young teenager joined the Junior Red Cross Nurses before becoming old enough to start full time training as a nurse in 1960 at the Newcastle General, and Ashington Hospitals as well as the Beulah House Maternity home in Blyth. When her three years training came to an end she answered an advertisement for NHS district nurses in the Blyth area and got one of the jobs.

She said: "There were several district nurses and we all had individual rounds. We had quite an area to cover, some of the places we had to visit were not so nice. There was one section we called Little Calcutta, for what reason I do not know, where some notorious families lived. We made sure if we had to call there that we were not alone.

Dorothy Hartshorne – after having qualified.

"That area was frequented by habitual criminals. On one occasion a doctor who was called out to an emergency there found when he returned to his car it had been put on blocks and the four wheels stolen."

Dorothy also recalled the time when it was possible to have an operation in Blyth at the Thomas Knight Memorial Hospital with specialist surgeons being brought in from other hospitals. "It was sad when we lost those facilities when it was closed down as it was an inconvenience to the town."

She also remembers having to treat Russian sailors in the Missions to Seamen in Stanley Street who were discharged from Thomas Knight to convalesce after being treated for whatever illness or disease they had. Their ships had, in the meantime sailed, and they had to stay at the Missions until the vessels returned. The district nurses also had to deal with children some of whom were sent to the Infectious diseases hospital at Monkeys Island, along the Links.

While Dorothy was a highly efficient nurse she proved not to be so efficient when it came to driving a car. "The NHS provided motor transport for the nurses and you could use the cars if you could drive. I couldn't and after sitting several tests I still could not pass," she said. This meant she had to use a bicycle every day to cover her rounds which stretched from Bebside to Seaton Sluice and all for the princely sum, in the early days, of £49 a month.

Dorothy Hartshorne in retirement.

District nurses were primarily involved in home nursing, changing dressings, giving insulin injections and the like but they were also used to provide information for the social services in the town.

"If we visited a house where we found some help was needed because of conditions we had to report it to the relevant department in Tweed House," she said. "Some of the houses, where elderly and children lived, were without power and were reported as they used candles, always a fire menace, as their only light source.

"A visit to Tweed House was not relished because of the impertinent attitude of some of the staff towards our reports. On occasions what we regarded as needing urgent action took to us what appeared to be an inordinate delay."

Dorothy said she thoroughly enjoyed the work but not one part of the job - the laying out of bodies and wrapping them in shrouds after death in homes on their visiting list.

Black Geordie – Scary Man

In the 2012 edition of Blyth Memories we told the story of Black Geordie, whose name was used by mothers to scare their children to behaving themselves.

His name was Geordie Hales and he came to Blyth as a waif from North Shields at the age of 12 in 1885. He lived in a stable along the Links and became a regular sight in the town, unkempt and unwashed. He got money by entertaining in pubs and the circus which stood on the site of the Wallaw Cinema.

One of his favourite tricks was to sit on the floor of the pub and sing the song Grace Darling as he pretended to row a boat. Unfortunately some of the onlookers used the performance to splash him with beer, impersonating the waves, but he did not seem to mind.

But he was held in such regard that when he joined up in the First World War townsfolk sent him parcels at the front. Anyhow following the publication I was sent a photograph of Black Geordie wearing a coat believed to have been given to him by Lt. Col. Nicholas I. Wright D.S.O. the managing director of Wrights Timber Yard and I thought it only right (pardon the pun) that it be kept for posterity.

A Puzzlement

I am hoping dear reader one of you may be able to throw light on this picture of a group in the Twenties, believed to be from the Blyth area, going under the name of The Buzzboys. Elderly musicians in the town are unable to help although it is possible that the trombonist was a Billy McCabe – his living relatives believe so. I was tipped off that it was a group which was formed at the United Bus Depot but not so. The setting of the picture appears to be in a room in a public house, again, after so many years not identifiable, as there are no pubs in Blyth which to my knowledge sell OXO! I hope someone is able to solve this puzzlement.